CW00557114

I Put Pants On For This?: Stories in Defense of Staying Home

Jackson Banks

Published by Jackson Banks, 2022.

I PUT PANTS ON FOR THIS?: STORIES IN DEFENSE OF STAYING HOME

First edition. July 19, 2022.

Copyright © 2022 Jackson Banks.

ISBN: 979-8201048952

Written by Jackson Banks.

Table of Contents

I Went to Cuba, and All I Got Was This Lousy Voodoo Curse

———

What was the first vacation you can remember taking as a kid? I bet it was Disney World. A lot of kids go to Disney World on their first vacation. Crammed into the family minivan, they excitedly ask, "Are we there yet?" over and over again. The anticipation of meeting Mickey and Minnie grows stronger by the mile. Upon arrival, they ride the Tea Cups and Pirates of the Caribbean and get the song from It's A Small World lodged in their brains for the duration of the trip. Mouse ears adorn their head as they wander the most magical place on earth.

What was the first vacation I can remember as a kid? Beaufort, South Carolina. That's not so bad, right? Sure, it doesn't have Mickey or Minnie or Pluto or Space Mountain, but it does have beaches and history. South Carolina's low country has lighthouses, dolphin-watching charters, and an old fort. And you would be right if that's what we did.

There was no gate to the Magic Kingdom with Cinderella's castle looming in the background when we arrived at my first vacation destination. Instead of reading "Happiest Celebration on Earth," the banner welcoming us read "We Make Marines."

Soldiers standing at attention decked in camouflage and armed with assault rifles greeted us at the front gate to Parris Island Marine Recruit Depot. A cold salute by a blank-faced sentry guard greeted us rather than a warm "Welcome!" by some college intern in mouse ears.

Aladdin was the most popular Disney movie at the time, and the song "A Whole New World" was all over the radio. I bet it was all over Disney World as well. I wouldn't know, because the only music I got to hear on our family vacation was the a cappella of a recruit platoon harmoniously chanting on their morning run. "Well, I don't know, but I've been told, Eskimo pussy is mighty cold. Sound off. One Two. Sound off. Three Four."

Seeing the recruits race through the obstacle course was pretty fun. It was like watching *American Ninja Warrior* decades before the show ever aired on television. There was something more raw and brutal without the bright colors and television lights. Most of the contestants on the television show also don't cry throughout the course as some muscular drill sergeant screams at them and calls them maggots and pieces of shit. My elementary school vocabulary was growing exponentially.

As you know, Peter Pan is one of Disney's most classic characters. He and his sidekick, Tinkerbell, are constantly fighting their Neverland nemesis Captain Hook. Unless your childhood was even more deprived than mine, you know Captain Hook got his name because an alligator took his hand, and he replaced the missing hand with a hook. There were alligators at Parris Island as well. I never saw them, but I know this to be a fact because of story time with Dad during our vacation.

"When I was a recruit here," he began just before bedtime, "things were horrible. Not at all as nice as you see them now. These recruits get a phone call a week. What a luxury! These recruits get subjected only to verbal abuse! Hell, our assess were literally kicked during training!"

"Okay..." I said while wearing my Batman pajamas.

"It was so bad, in fact, that one of my fellow recruits tried to escape in the middle of the night. He went AWOL. That means Absent Without Leave. Ran right off the base!"

"Okay..."

"Do you know what happened to him? Do you?"

"No, Dad."

"Neither do we! Because they never found him! Rumor was he ran off the base and into the swamp, and he was torn apart by the alligators. They never found a trace of him anywhere!"

A pause.

"All right, well, story time is over, Son. Good night."

"Um, good night?"

The lights went out.

Most Disney vacations end in grand fashion with the Electrical Parade and fireworks. Our family vacation ended with a trip to the firing range and recruit graduation. Close enough, I suppose. We returned home to Marine Corps Air Station Cherry Point the next day.

Base housing on Cherry Point was modest and simple. Our government-supplied home was one of the first that I can remember, and the base itself was where I was born and spent most of the early years of my childhood. There were woods with a trail system near the home where my friends and I would spend most of our days after school and on the weekends.

Often, we would pretend to be Marines like our fathers. We would also pretend to be explorers. Hunting Sasquatch and other mythical beasts was a favorite pastime. We were always looking for adventure in whatever we were doing.

I remember well the evening when I knew this world would end. My father walked through the front door of our home in his camouflage fatigues carrying a slip of paper. He had been given orders to another assignment, and we were to accompany him. The destination: Guantanamo Bay, Cuba.

I was eight years old and thus had no idea where Guantanamo Bay was or what a Cuba was. My mother pulled out a small globe we had in our house and showed me the Island of Cuba, pointing to the southeastern corner where we would soon make our home.

I was angry at first. I did not want to leave Cherry Point. My school was there, my friends were there, and my fort was in the woods. Every year you could see the Navy Blue Angels flying over our home practicing for the annual air show. It was all I knew and all I wanted to know.

I calmed down after a little while and thought more about where we were going to be living. I was a big fan of pirates, like a lot of young boys living on the North Carolina coast. I began to dream of high seas adventure and buried treasure. I was about to become a modern-day pirate of the Caribbean. Who cares if I was only eight years old? It would be the ultimate fun-filled adventure.

My mother and I left for Cuba in November 1992. My father had gone down several months before us to begin his duties on base and to set up the base housing for us once a home became available. Before we left for me to begin my career as a pirate, we had to leave MCAS Cherry Point and drive north to Norfolk, Virginia, to catch our transport plane to Guantanamo Bay.

It was bitterly cold the morning we left, and we had to wake in the middle of the night since our flight to Guantanamo was before sunrise. This was the military, after all, and you will be subjected to unpleasantness and bureaucratic nonsense for no reason regardless of whether you are a solider or a civilian dependent.

When it was time to leave, we filed into the plane and took our moderately uncomfortable seats.

The morning we left was freezing, and there was a light snow in Norfolk. I was dressed appropriately. Since I was only eight years old at the time, I didn't fully understand the concept of layering one's outfit.

When we finally landed in Cuba and stepped off the plane, I instantly started sweating and felt like I had been punched in the face by the fires of hell itself. "Welcome to your new home," Satan laughed from the great beyond. It may have just been Fidel Castro on a loud speaker. I was too young to know for sure.

The airfield was across the bay from the rest of the base. After we met my father in the air terminal, we caught a bus down a short road to the bay where a ferry boat waited to take us from the westward side where the airfield was located to the leeward side where the rest of the base awaited us.

The ferry transported us across crystal clear turquoise waters. If you looked off the side of the ferry, you could see all manner of tropical sea life through the water. Dolphins even played off the bow and in the wake. So I was told. I passed out from heat stroke long before the boat left the dock.

This was to be our home for the next two years. Forty-five square miles of military base that we were not allowed to leave; most of it the bay itself, restricted military buildings, or the western hemisphere's largest field of land mines at the time. Orientation to the base included a listing of restaurants, activities, and the locations of the beaches. Important knowledge was shared as well, such as a warning to check our shoes before we put them on. A man had died on the ferry because a scorpion had crawled in his boot and stung him repeatedly; he thought he was merely stepping on a rock in his shoe.

In other words, we had arrived in paradise.

━━━━━━

Base housing in Guantanamo Bay was radically different from the housing at Cherry Point. The one-story bungalow-style home was made of drab cinder block. The flat roof was made of concrete as well. The windows were cheap, and the only air conditioner providing respite from the sweltering equatorial climate was an ancient window unit. The house looked like one of those bunkers the Japanese used in World War II, only above ground.

But the view! Palm trees. Caribbean Sea. A tropical paradise right outside our windows!

No. My father was an enlisted Marine. That means the military provided us with housing because they were obligated to, not because they cared to. The nicer homes were reserved for officers and those who were lucky. My family has never been known for our luck.

We did have a view, though. Directly across our front lawn and the street was a tangled mess of brush. Guantanamo Bay, for whatever reason, is a desert-like portion of Cuba. There is no lush jungle or charming seaside villa. It's a barren, dry, and rough-and-tumble place that resembles more of Texas than it does Florida. Beyond the brush was more brush, and beyond that in the far distance was the fence.

The fence surrounded the entire base—a never-ending stretch of tall chain link topped with barbed wire, separating freedom from communism. Dotted at intervals along the fence line on both sides were guard towers where bored sentries suffered in the heat while sweating through their uniforms. Only .50 caliber machine guns pointed at the other side kept them company.

Beyond the fence in front of our house was a mountain and a Cuban town. Perched atop the mountain was a Cuban outpost. There were Cuban military personnel who were watching our every move the entire time.

The house was not without its charm, however. For one thing, it came with its own entertainment. Every night at precisely 9:00 p.m., I would look out the window at the Cuban town beyond the fence line with their lights twinkling in the night. Then, suddenly, the town would go dark all at once, and it was swallowed into the night. The Cuban government shut off the power to the entire city to ration and conserve electricity. This was communism.

Then there was the local wildlife we shared the neighborhood with as well. Every now and then, a banana rat would wander across the lawn or be seen in the brush across the street. Formally known as Hutias, banana rats are large rodents that can grow up to three feet in length and resemble a mix between a guinea pig and an opossum. Although they are hunted for food in communist Cuba, in Guantanamo Bay, there is actually an overpopulation because of abundant food sources and a lack of natural predators. There were also large frogs that would for some reason commit suicide by jumping into our outside dryer vent, getting lodged there until they died of starvation or suffocated. The roaches were the size of an adult's hand.

Then one night I heard my mother screaming. She had gone to use the bathroom in the middle of the night and heard a clicking, crawling sound coming from the bathtub next to the commode. When she looked in, she was greeted by a scorpion that had managed to crawl up through the plumbing and drain. There were tarantulas as well.

As welcoming and cozy as our new home was, it was eventually time to venture out and explore the base.

Our first excursion was to the beach. I'm sure you're picturing the Caribbean beaches you've seen on television or been to yourself. White sand, coconuts, palm trees, a blissful breeze, and the soothing sound of the waves. A place where you can escape all of your problems and relax without a worry in the world.

This was not that type of beach. The "sand" was all crushed coral and rock. One required shoes at all times at this beach unless one was professional Shakti mat user or masochist. There were palm trees and shelters for picnics, however. This is where we began our first beach trip.

This is a good time to mention that Guantanamo Bay is home to the rare and endangered *Cyclura nubila*. They are better known as the Cuban Rock Iguana, or Cuban Ground Iguana. These lizards are all over the base and surrounding area and love to make their homes near the shore and sea. They can grow anywhere between three and five feet in length.

My dad brought hot dogs to grill, and we had chips to go with them. I loved chips and hot dogs as a kid. Do you know who else loved chips and hot dogs? The Cuban Rock Iguana. The iguanas were not shy about making their love for this human delicacy known and would often come right up to you and beg like a scaly, ugly puppy. Feeding them was discouraged, however.

The iguanas did not get that memo. They encouraged you to feed them food. They attempted to take it if you did not voluntarily feed them. They would also chase you. Note: iguanas run fast. Thus, one of my first adventures as a pirate of the Caribbean was not finding buried treasure but being chased down the beach with a hot dog in my hand by a four-foot-long descendant of the dinosaurs.

Once I surrendered my lunch to the reptilian bullies, it was time to go for a swim in the warm waters of the Caribbean. I planned to snorkel and look at all the tropical fish and splash my worries away.

"You have to be careful," my dad said.

"I know, Dad. I always am."

"No, I mean more careful than back home in North Carolina. There's a lot of tiger sharks, bull sharks, and barracuda in these waters. Take your watch off. I know it's waterproof, but the metal is flashy, and they might mistake your hand for a fish."

"Um…okay," I said. I had visions of becoming a real-life Captain Hook.

"Also, you need to watch the current. No drifting with it. You need to make sure you stay near where you go in."

"Why?"

"Do you see that fence line?" My dad pointed about fifty yards down the beach where the base's permitter fence ended in the ocean.

"Yes."

"Do you see that guy up in that tower?" My dad pointed to the Cuban guard tower just on the other side of the fence and slightly down the beach.

"Yes." I waved to the Cuban solider looking down at the beach with his machine gun.

"Don't do that! He's not our friend! He's a goddamn communist!"

I stopped waving.

"Well, anyway, like I was saying, don't let the current take you over the fence line, or that commie bastard will shoot you. Do you want to get shot?"

"I guess not."

———————————

Cuba was not all fun and games. The rainy season tended to flood the base to the point that Marines would need to sandbag the perimeter of the elementary school I attended. The base commander would test our hurricane preparedness by cutting power and all essential utilities on base, usually on the hottest day of the month. Occasionally, a loud percussion could be heard in the distance when an errant banana rat wandered onto the minefield and triggered a mine. The list goes on.

The Morale, Welfare and Recreation Department maintained stables and bridle trails on the base for families to use to provide a respite from the stress of daily island life. My parents thought this would be a good way to have some fun family time and see more of the base in the initial months of our tour.

The bridle trails wound through the base's backcountry and up the back of the mountains in the center of the base, which provided a great view of the bay and the sea.

We had never ridden horses before, and the stable personnel looked skeptical when we arrived to saddle up. Apparently, shorts and flip-flops are proper attire for anywhere on the island except the stables and the back of a horse. So we left, got changed into jeans and proper shoes, and headed back to the stables with just a few minutes to spare before our guided tour was set to begin.

I had visions of Zorro and The Lone Ranger going through my preadolescent head while the stable boys took care to select just the right horse for me. I was sure it would be a majestic mustang or a handsome Arabian. Instead, it was an Elmer.

The horse's name was Blue. Or perhaps Glue. It's hard to remember this far removed. I can assure you that Glue would be the most appropriate name for the horse.

Although the average life span of a horse is roughly twenty-five to thirty years, I estimate Glue was approximately 197 years old. He meandered out of the stable with the stable boy holding his bridle tight. This was unnecessary, however, as Glue moved so slowly that even if he did decide to run, I'm quite sure an arthritic turtle could catch him.

I reached up to pet his snout and realized that Glue had only one eye with a patch over the missing one. If nothing else, at least I had a pirate horse on a Caribbean island for my first ride.

The stable boy quickly placed a saddle on Glue and helped me get on top of him. After some preliminary instruction, we were on our way with a guide and a few other families on the base.

The initial meandering down the trail was nothing like I thought it would be after watching all of the old John Wayne movies. We seemed to be moving at an imperceptibly slow pace, looking at the dirt, sand, and shrubbery around the trail, most of which were various forms of cacti.

We eventually came to a wider and more open area. Our guide, without warning, suddenly accelerated his horse into a cantor, and the herd followed after him. Much to my surprise, old Glue began to run as well. I was excited and felt like a cowboy.

The excitement lasted precious few moments and gave way to terror as I found myself airborne, arms and legs extended like Superman flying, only my body was sideways instead of my chest being parallel to the ground. I came down with a thud on the dusty trail and struggled to regain my breath as I wiped horse shit from my nose.

I looked back at old Glue. He was now stopped along with the other horses, and the saddle that had been hastily thrown on him was hanging underneath his belly.

The guide approached and asked if I was okay, and I nodded since I still couldn't take a full breath.

"Sorry about that," the guide said. "It looks like the stable boy didn't put the saddle on tight enough. That sometimes happens with Blue. If you linger around him too long, he'll kick ya."

I stared at the guide, then at Glue, and couldn't seem to understand what he was talking about.

"He's a tough old guy. One time when I was riding him, he got angry with me and threw me right off. I landed in a cactus." The guide lifted up his shirt to show the small round scars from the needles on his abdomen. "So," continued the guide, "you got lucky by just landing in some horse shit."

"Walk it off, Shit Face," Dad said helpfully.

It would be a while before I outlived my new nickname.

Eating out was a challenge in Guantanamo Bay. There were essentially four options to choose from on the entire base: the ubiquitous McDonald's; the hot dog cart in the Exchange entryway; a pizza place; and The Cuban Club. The Cuban Club was the base favorite, as it was something other than fast food.

As you may expect, the specialties of the The Cuban Club were traditional Caribbean food. There were Cuban sandwiches, fresh-caught fish and seafood, and black beans and rice. Jerk chicken was also on the menu. In fact, it was on every menu, even at the elementary school cafeteria where we ate the dish at least three times a week. If the old adage "you are what you eat" is true, then jerk chicken is the reason I'm a jerk today.

One day after a jerk chicken lunch at the school cafeteria, we had recess where a scheduled show-and-tell session occurred. This show-and-tell theme was centered not on the kids but on the other aspect of Guantanamo Bay that was even more impossible to escape than the jerk chicken: the military.

As we stood on the playground in the sweltering Cuban heat and humidity, we began to hear a rumble off in the distance. Suddenly, camouflage was everywhere as a convoy of Marine Corps Humvees drove down the road and entered our schoolyard. Dozen of Marines, most with assault rifles, jumped out.

Over the next few hours, the Marines demonstrated what would happen if the communists on the other side of the fence ever threatened to steal our freedom. We watched with excitement the exercises and demonstrations before us and could hardly contain ourselves when we were enlisted to participate.

First, I was shown how to shoot a .45 caliber handgun accurately. Then, I crawled up into a Humvee and fired off the .50 caliber mounted gun at some unsuspecting vultures circling the sun above. Of course, the guns were shooting blanks so no one was actually hurt in the process.

But what does one do if there is no gun available? The Marines had this covered as well. A sergeant pulled me and a friend out of a line of boys for the next demonstration.

"Now, what we're going to do is have a hand-to-hand combat demonstration," announced the sergeant. My friend and I looked at each other nervously.

After having us demonstrate some basic self defense techniques, the sergeant turned to us and said, "What I'm about to show you next is something very effective. But you have to promise me that you will never, ever use it unless your life is in danger. Do you promise?"

"We promise," my friend and I answered in unison with fingers crossed behind our backs.

"Okay. Now, this is how you kill someone with a single blow of your palm," the sergeant continued. Our eyes widened with awe as we were shown the technique. I still contend to this day it was the best show-and-tell ever.

———

Generally speaking, the dangerous creatures that inhabit Guantanamo Bay stayed in their respective ecosystems. The iguanas, scorpions, tarantulas, banana rats, and horses stayed outside in the hot and humid landscape. The sharks and barracuda stayed in the bay and the ocean. The soldiers stayed in their homes, barracks, depots, and offices.

Sure, occasionally the creatures would become adventurous and try to test the boundaries of nature. The iguanas would occasionally go swimming in the ocean. Scorpions would crawl up our shower drain. Soldiers would scuba dive in their off time.

Occasional adventure is fine and good for every living thing. But if it occurs once a year, every year it ceases to be occasional and instead becomes a tradition. A certain creature inhabiting Guantanamo Bay had a very annoying and smelly tradition.

Millions of crabs emerge from the area surrounding Guantanamo Bay each spring to make their way to the sea to mate. These crabs are not just on the beaches when they arrive, they are everywhere—the parks, the sidewalks, at the bottom of the community pools, on the schoolyard, and on the roads. An aerial view of the base would reveal a sea of crabs comparable to the sea of trees in the Amazon.

These were not small fiddler crabs. These were crabs the size of softballs. I know what you're thinking. You're thinking that sounds delicious, and you would be correct if this were any place other than Guantanamo Bay. These particular crabs contained a harmful toxin that prevents humans from eating them without dire consequences.

Getting around base became problematic and expensive since new tires were guaranteed expenditures. The crabs' shells shredded car tires. *Crunch. Crack. Crunch. Crack. Pop.*

Our backyards in base housing were generally the only safe place to be among the crab hoard moving about like zombies because they were surrounded by chain-link fences that made it virtually impossible for the crabs to gain access. This, like everything in life, was not foolproof.

One morning, I went out into the backyard to play when, suddenly, I heard a scratching sound coming from the other side of our shed. I went to investigate and found myself staring face-to-face with crustacean anger.

Like with people, and most other animals, crabs get angry when you stand between them and sex. Although I assumed I was just playing in my own backyard, this particular crab thought I was effectively cock blocking him, and he was intent on making his displeasure known.

The crab continued to stare at me angrily with his beady, lifeless black eyes. He began to click his pincers together rapidly. Anticipation of a fight hung in the air. Suddenly, the crab took the offensive position and advanced to attack.

Here is a thing about crabs that you probably already knew: they can move fast when they want.

Here is a thing about crabs that you may not have already known: they are arthropods, which is the extended animal family of which arachnids belong.

I screamed when the crab started charging just like I do when spiders decide they want to come after me. Loud and panicked.

I continued to run around my backyard in circles as I was chased by the horny crab for approximately five minutes. Eventually, I was able to slow it down by going around our large lime tree, which offered a straight shot to the back door. I ran as fast as my legs would carry me and found security and safety behind the door once back inside.

I listened to the crab scratch and click against the door for at least fifteen minutes before it realized I was safe in my people shell and he was free to move on and find a mate. I refused to leave the house for the remainder of the invasion.

The world's largest crab orgy ended, as do all good things. The crabs crawled back to whatever realm of hell they came from postcoital and presumably satisfied with themselves. Of course, they did not have the decency to clean up first and left thousands of their dead brethren smashed on our roadways and sidewalks.

Something had to clean up the crabs, and the circle of life brought enough seagulls to the point where the entire base looked like a scene from Alfred Hitchcock's *The Birds*. Insects claimed what the gulls did not. The base eventually stopped smelling like a rotting fish market, at least until the next year when the crabs got horny again.

I did not appreciate it at the time, but one of the greatest things about Guantanamo Bay was the exposure to different cultures that it offered. Jamaicans worked in various civil positions on the base, and Cubans that had worked on base prior to the embargo were allowed to continue coming each day and carrying out their jobs. These migrant workers lent their culture and insight to the base environment.

Haitians were also present on base, although they were not quite as lucky to have jobs or general freedom like the Jamaicans or even the communist Cubans. There had been a contingent of Haitian refugees housed in an internment camp on the base for several years before our arrival. Unauthorized personnel were not allowed to enter the camp or have contact with them.

The Haitians housed in the internment camp often became unhappy that they had fled the political, economic, and social turmoil of their homeland for a better life in the nearby United States only to find themselves indefinitely housed in what was essentially a prison. Often, the resident Haitians of the base would riot to demonstrate their displeasure.

These riots were almost never scheduled for a convenient time, which I suppose is the case with most riots. They almost always occurred in the middle of the night, and that meant I often was awoken by the phone ringing and my dad cussing and banging around while putting on his uniform at three in the morning. Guantanamo Bay may have been a Naval Base, but the Navy almost always sends in the Marines to fix its problems.

Over breakfast a few hours later, Dad would often tell us about his night. "Those sons of bitches were causing all kinds of problems, throwing blood and feces everywhere and at everyone."

I took another bite of my Fruit Loops.

"Then this one chick starts dancing around and chanting, throwing more blood and shit and chicken bones," Dad continued. "Apparently, she was chanting a voodoo curse."

"You had a voodoo curse put on you last night?" I asked.

"Not just me. Apparently, she cursed our whole family."

I finished my Fruit Loops and went to school.

I didn't know it at the time, but I wouldn't have to go to school much longer. Our school year on base ended toward the middle of June; however, at the beginning of May 1994, more and more "guests" began to arrive on base. During this time, thousands of refugees were fleeing both communist Cuba and Haiti, attempting to reach Florida.

These refugees were intercepted in Operation Sea Signal by the United States Navy and the Coast Guard. Not wanting to allow them onto the continental United States, the government sent them to Guantanamo Bay. A tent city was constructed on an old airfield. This was the founding of the now infamous Camp X-Ray.

Soon more and more naval ships and Coast Guard cutters began arriving in the bay bringing the refugees with them. My family would take occasional trips to Camp X-Ray to remind ourselves how fortunate we were to be Americans.

It was hard to imagine what it must have been like to live in a country you wanted to escape so badly that you would leave everything behind and risk your life to float on a raft of tires and scrap wood ninety or more miles across shark-infested seas.

Life continued essentially as normal on base except for the arrival of more and more refugees. At least for a while. One day, as I was in school daydreaming about some adventure while my teacher tried in vain to teach me long division, the principal's voice came over the intercom for an announcement.

"Attention, teachers and students. Today will be the last day of the school year. Please return all textbooks and clear out your belongings by the end of the day."

It was only May, and we still had more than a month left in the school year. My teacher stopped talking about long division and stood at the front of the classroom wide-eyed and stunned as twenty fourth graders jumped for joy at an early summer vacation.

We found out as the day went on that we were being shut down by the military because they needed our school buses to transport the ever-growing influx of refugees from the bay to Camp X-Ray. They needed our buses immediately, of course.

Ending the school year with a few hours' notice presented logistical concerns. For one, we students could not gradually clear out our desks and lockers and wind down the year in an orderly fashion. Some of us, like myself, had only a small backpack and were now faced with carrying much more than would fit back home with us. With no buses, of course.

Our house was more than a mile from the school, and those of us who lived further away would be allowed to go to the school's office to call our parents and arrange for rides. Imagine being one of those parents to receive a phone call unexpectedly informing you that your child's school was closing effective immediately. I could hear my father screaming from his office a few miles away already.

I entered the office where the scene was chaotic because the office staff were also taken by surprise by the close of school. The frazzled secretary plopped the phone down on the desk in front of me and walked away to attend to some bureaucratic red tape.

I stared at the phone not knowing what to do. I was a child of the late eighties and early nineties and thus grew up with a touch-tone phone. The phone in front of me was a rotary phone that I was quite sure predated Fidel Castro.

I picked up the handset and with my other hand pressed the numbers with my finger. No beep, boop, beep. No ringing. Nothing. I pressed the number again, and again nothing happened. I stared at the phone.

I looked around for the secretary, and she was still nowhere to be seen. I returned the handset, not knowing how to use the antique in front of me, and walked out of the office defeated.

I eventually began the long trek back home in the Cuban heat carrying a full backpack and an armful of other personal belongings. The weight became heavier with each passing step in the midday sun. I was sure the Marines were used to this situation, but I was still just a kid, and while I had been to Parris Island, it was just on vacation.

Sweating and thirsty, and with arms shaking, I was ready to give up and just sit down on the sidewalk and wait for someone to drive by. I had seen a movie once where someone hitchhiked, so I was pretty sure I might be able to try that and not get murdered. I stopped walking and was preparing to put my possessions down when I noticed movement out of the corner of my eye.

A large scorpion was crawling toward me. The pinchers outstretched and tail raised above its armored body, it appeared to be moving fast and effortlessly in the sweltering heat. I subsequently moved just as fast as I ran all the way back to the house.

Cuba did not turn out to be the Caribbean paradise I had imagined it only two years before. It was an oppressively hot wasteland filled with giant lizards, large crabs, scorpions, tarantulas, sharks, barracuda, communism, land mines, and guard towers with machine guns. There was also a memorial to Christopher Columbus.

I had looked at the memorial at the ferry landing many times over those two years. Columbus landed in Guantanamo Bay on April 30, 1494, during his second voyage to the New World looking for gold. He and his crew spent just a single night in the bay and left the next morning never to return. I couldn't help but wonder why he even bothered to spend the night.

Our time in Cuba was drawing to a close. In the summer months, my father came home once more in his camouflage fatigues carrying another slip of paper. We were to ship out for Camp LeJune in November. There was no trepidation on my part about leaving Guantanamo Bay as there had been with Cherry Point, and, although it was only June, I wasted no time packing up my bedroom. I was ready to board the plane by that very same weekend.

Luck was on our side for once, and we did not have to wait till November. Some strings were pulled, and we rode the ferry for the last time to the airfield in early August to catch our plane back stateside.

Feeling the acceleration of the plane press me into my seat was one of the most exciting moments I can remember from childhood. The sudden drop the plane took off the cliff at the end of the runway before gaining altitude was one of the scariest.

Next stop: North Carolina.

Three days after our departure from Guantanamo Bay, an order was issued by the base commander due to the ever-increasing numbers of refugees coming onto the base. The desalinization plant could no longer provide enough fresh water for everyone on base, and all nonessential personnel and civilians were to be evacuated from the base and sent back stateside.

Had we not gotten out when we did, our possessions and future would be in limbo like a majority of the rest of the base. It appeared that whatever voodoo curse had been placed on my family that one night had lost its potency.

That Time Exercise Almost Killed Me

J im lives in Colorado. As such, he's generally annoying. He doesn't eat sugar or carbs. He bikes to work and runs up 14,000-foot mountains each week for exercise. He has zero body fat and looks like a model from the cover of one of those fitness magazines. Jim is the type of man who may as well just spell his name "Gym."

I, on the other hand, live in North Carolina. I eat sugar and carbs. I drive to work and hike up the fourteen stairs to the second story of my home for exercise each week. I am overweight by thirty pounds and look like a model in a before picture from a Weight Watchers advertisement. I am the type of man who may as well just spell his name "Chipotle."

Thinking back, I cannot remember exactly why I told Jim I would run a 50k race with him in the desert outside of Las Vegas. I can only assume that his timing corresponded nicely with my consumption of whiskey. Nevertheless, I did agree; and I am a man of my word if nothing else.

Months of thinking about training were expended before the trip out west. This was followed by weeks of anxiety and days of panicked running in the hope of being ready for whatever lie ahead on the 50k trail when it was time to race.

We flew to Las Vegas two days before the race so we could get acclimated to the climate and altitude, to obtain food, and whatever else we would need to be ready the morning of the race.

Jim had no problem getting acclimated since he lived in Colorado and at higher elevation. I, however, live in Raleigh and am close to sea level. The 3,000-foot difference would make the race only harder.

Motivation was not my problem. I was greeted at McCarran International Airport by a neon glow and a sea of slot machines after disembarking from my plane after a short flight. The electronic noises from the machines many travelers were sitting in front of, mindlessly pulling the levers, echoed through the terminal. I was ready to run 50k and beyond back to Raleigh after taking in the scene.

I meandered through the slot machines and the mixed hoards, half of which were arriving in Las Vegas bright-eyed and ready to strike it rich or party, while the other half were departing shell-shocked, hungover, and broke.

I found an airport bar and waited for Jim's flight to arrive from Colorado. The bar was empty. I picked a stool and ordered a beer.

Some stupidly nonsensical sporting event was on the giant TV mounted on the wall above the whiskey bottles. I believe people call it "soccer." Hundreds if not thousands in the city were also probably watching it and losing money on bets. Even if they were not betting, they were losing anyway because they were watching the game to begin with.

I stared mindlessly at the TV for half of a beer and then turned my attention to more exciting things like the pictures on the wall and the people wandering down the concourse to their gates. This may sound boring, but sitting alone with my thoughts in a bar or coffee shop while people watching is one of my favorite pastimes. The bartender had other plans for my time in his establishment, however.

I have been told by others my entire life that I have a generally grumpy-appearing face, yet people always try to approach me and start a conversation. The bartender was no exception. Despite my normal body language shouting "leave me alone" to anyone who can see, the bartender decided to strike up a conversation.

"First time in Vegas?"

"Yes," I replied.

"You here to gamble?"

"No."

"You here to see a show?"

"No."

"Bachelor party?"

"Nope."

I tried to estimate how long this guessing game would continue before he cut to the chase.

"You here for the convention?"

"No."

He paused for a moment and considered his next move.

"You a sports fan?" he asked.

"Absolutely not," I said with a chuckle.

"What brings you to town then?"

I took another sip of my beer as I considered whether to pretend my flight was getting ready to leave.

"I'm here to run a 50k race in Bootleg Canyon in a few days."

The bartender looked upon my obesity, and his eyes grew wide.

"Really?" he asked in disbelief.

"Really."

"How far is 50k?"

"It's about 31 miles."

His mouth was now agape, and his eyes grew even wider.

"Why would you want to do something like that?" he asked.

"I'm not entirely sure," I replied.

The bartender prattled on about how he hates running but loves CrossFit for enough time for me to drink another beer. As he continued rambling, I glanced toward the entrance of the bar and mercifully saw Jim coming down the concourse. I paid my tab and left.

"Good luck in your race," the bartender said with a smirk as I walked out the door.

The next day, Jim and I had planned to scout out the race course and gather whatever food at a grocery store we would need for the morning of the race and any supplements we might need to get us through the 31 miles of running we had paid good hard-earned money to suffer through. But first, we needed breakfast.

Once we left our hotel on The Strip and ventured away from the casinos, it wasn't hard to find a handful of diners to choose from. Most of the establishments looked like they had not see a health inspector in years. We ultimately settled on the one that looked somewhat cleaner than a public restroom.

Jim doesn't eat sugar or carbohydrates, so I'm not entirely sure what he managed to order for breakfast. The diner's executive chef likely yanked a cactus up by the roots out back and threw it on a plate as far as I can recall. As for me, I went with a sensible, healthy option: biscuits and gravy.

We drove up to Bootleg Canyon following breakfast. The weather could not have been more perfect. It was a sunny day with almost no humidity, and since it was November, it was neither too hot nor too cold.

A welcome sign greeted us in the canyon with decorations reminiscent of a Mad Max movie. The trails on the crudely drawn map were named to make visitors feel comfortable and invited: Armageddon, Kevorkian, Widow Maker, and Reaper, just to name a few. Everything was rust-colored and dusty. "What the hell have I gotten myself into?" I whispered to myself.

After consulting the map, we continued up the dirt road to the top of a ridge overlooking the entire canyon. In the distance, the Las Vegas skyline was visible, and on the other side of the ridge, the sun sparkled off Lake Mead. Glancing over the canyon, a vast network of narrow dirt trails were visible as far as the eye could see. Mountain bikers would come into view only to vanish suddenly behind another ridge. From our high vantage point, the race course did not look as arduous as I had expected. A sense of calm began to envelope me. It would dissipate the following morning.

Our next stop was the grocery store. It was a chain Jim shopped at regularly in Colorado. I don't remember the name of it, but you know the type. It was one of those boutique grocery stores where everything is organic, free-range, or kale flavored and one in which granola describes not only the bulk of their cereal aisle but also the bulk of the customers. We split up to do our respective shopping.

I went in search of my standard grocery fare and wandered the aisles aimlessly as I marveled at the selection of healthy food and the exceptionally high prices. Where were the Doritos? Frosted Flakes? Why was all of the so-called milk plant-based and not from a cow? These were important questions I was never able answer.

We rendezvoused near the checkout aisles that were staffed exclusively by millennials wearing flannel and adorned with numerous piercings and tattoos, both the men and the women.

Jim had predictably chosen options someone into extreme fitness would choose: bean sprouts, cage-free organic eggs, and an avocado. I had in my basket lemon-flavored yogurt, vegan gluten-free chocolate chip cookies, and organic gummy bears for what would possibly be my last meal on Earth.

We arrived in Bootleg Canyon the morning of the race and pulled into the same dirt parking lot from the day before. I was unusually nervous for just before a race, and I had to keep taking deep breaths since my life was continually flashing before my eyes.

The race organizers decided to make the 50k something trail runners call a "Fat Ass" style of race. This essentially means there is no water or food support along the course, and the route itself is unmarked. We were given written directions on where to turn during the race.

I am not sure where the term "Fat Ass" comes from in trail running, nor anything of its history. This leads me to suspect that it may have been coined for this race because I had registered to run.

I lined up at the start line next to Jim and other runners who resembled Olympians and professional athletes of various disciplines. All looked determined, calm, and ready to conquer the course in front of us. None of them looked like they ate gummy bears for breakfast. I looked as nervous as a death row inmate making his way to the electric chair.

We waited for what seemed like an eternity, and suddenly the starter pistol went off. It was time to begin our short 31 mile jog.

The first few hundred yards after crossing the start line were not so bad. It was mostly downhill and easy terrain, and I felt quite confident in myself for the first time since agreeing to run the race.

"I can do this. I will do this," I kept chanting to myself. "31 miles is not so far." I laughed out loud at this.

Then came the first turn. I knew I had become lost already on the unmarked course, because the downhill and easy terrain were gone. I was doing so well running, I somehow had run all the way to Nepal and was now standing at Everest Base Camp. I came to a complete halt as my neck craned straight up.

I stood at the base of a near vertical 3,000-foot mountain of rock, dirt, and switchbacks. Other runners were bounding up the trail as if they were mountain goats on steroids.

I thought briefly about just turning back and walking to the start line, but I realized that, too, would be uphill at this point. So I took a deep breath and began my ascent at a reasonable running pace. I was well behind the other runners at this point but not in last place as many probably expected. There were two septuagenarians walking the race behind me with their Jack Russell terrier.

I was not able to run up the entire ascent. I thought I had made a good effort in the twenty strides I was able to take before my body forced me to start walking. As I climbed further up the switchbacks, I began to resemble an eighty-year-old man, hunched over and struggling to move as the trail became steeper and steeper.

The septuagenarians were improvidently shortening the distance between us. At the top of the mountain, some kid was sounding a

Vuvuzela to cheer us along with some other spectators. This did nothing to improve the situation. I wanted to lay down and wait for the vultures. But against my better judgment, I kept putting one foot in front of the other.

I finally reached the summit and took a second to relish the fact that I was still alive and surrounded by the breathtaking beauty of dusty dirt and rock. I looked at my GPS watch: 2.5 miles. Only 28.3 more miles to go! All but a few runners had disappeared from view on the unmarked course at this point.

The course made its way along the summit of the mountain, and the trail became even more complex. Dirty, gravelly, single track gave way to rocks, boulders, and steep drop-offs. I slowed to a barely noticeable trot for fear of ending up broken and bloody in the canyons below.

The septuagenarians were still gaining on me, moving quite adeptly along the course. A few other runners who appeared to be in their late fifties were a little ways up the trail.

At some point, I became aware that I had a running partner. No, not Jim. He was long gone and out of eyesight, leaving me for dead in the desert like the friend he is.

It was the Jack Russell terrier. He stayed by my side for eight miles before he left me behind. For much of that distance, he matched my labored pace with a smile that conveyed, "This isn't a big deal! This is fun! We're having fun!" in that stupid way dogs smile. He did not have a collar, so I gave him a name myself. I named him Bastard.

The trail eventually descended into a relatively flat valley shortly after Bastard left me to rejoin his owners. This was pleasant terrain to run along. The dirt was soft yet compact enough not to make it difficult, and desert sage lined the path giving off a nice aroma.

I began to regain hope that I would not be dinner for vultures at some point in the day. The hope and lack of elevation allowed me to gain some speed, and I started to run fast again. I even passed some other runners, which caused me to become even more excited.

At some point in the valley, I rounded a curve and saw more mountains ahead of me. Unfortunately, one could plainly see the path ascended into these mountains. These were not as high as Everest at the beginning of the course. These mountains looked more like Denali or K2. I stopped again, huffing and puffing and questioning my life choices. As I stood there, I looked around and saw Las Vegas off in the distance. I closed my eyes and began tapping my heels together, muttering "There's no place like Las Vegas" over and over.

There truly is no place like Las Vegas. It's a beautiful oasis of a city with wonderful architecture intermixed with natural beauty. The people are well dressed and typically high fashion, and cultural wonders abound.

This, of course, is bullshit. Las Vegas is what would result if Times Square and Myrtle Beach, South Carolina, had a bastard love child with behavioral issues. The entire city is bathed in neon light promising riches and performances by pop stars that no longer have a career. The tourists of the city throng the street, wandering aimlessly in a myriad of Wal-Mart's finest clothing selections. Some complete their outfit with the ever-stylish fanny pack. The city's motto is, "What happens in Vegas stays in Vegas." Thank God for that.

Still, I would have given anything to be on The Strip at that moment. I opened my eyes, and instead of staring at the Bellagio, I was still staring at the mountains ahead. Dorothy is full of shit.

I began to put one foot in front of the other once again, seeing no other option to escape the race. Unlike the mountains at the beginning of the course, I was now in an area of the canyon that was mostly foothills, a constant up-and-down roller coaster.

In one of the canyons, I came across a rather peculiar curiosity. In the middle of a dried-out creek bed sat a lone barstool with a chair back. On the weathered and dust-covered bar stool was a rib cage and a few scattered bones.

I became worried and began to yell at the stool: "Jim, is that you? Oh, Jim. Why did you wait for me to finish, Jim? I'm fat, Jim! You should have known it would take me forever to complete the course! Why am I out here?"

"Excuse me, sir. Are you running the race as well?" came a call from behind me.

It was a group of four other runners. They were middle-aged and looked healthy, like they should not have been coming from behind me in this race. I thought I had remembered seeing them at the start line before they bounded off far ahead of me like gazelles.

"Yes," I replied.

"Oh, great!" Their apparent leader continued, "We got lost on the trail somewhere. We took a wrong turn in the valley until we realized none of the landmarks matched the directions. Who are you talking to? Are you all right?"

"I'm fine. I was just thinking aloud, wondering if I was going the wrong way as well." I thought it better to let them think I was an idiot like them than crazy for talking to dead Jim.

The five of us began running again through the mountains and ravines. Up, down, up, down. Left foot, right foot, left foot, right foot. Up, down, up, down. Running is so monotonous. I'm not sure why anyone does it.

After what felt like forever, but was probably only a short distance, we came across a horrible site in the trail. A fork. We had the option of going right or left.

The five of us stood there looking right, then looking left, and then looking right once more. Several of us consulted the directions we were given, but no one seemed to be able to find where we were on the course.

It has been both my life's curse and gift that people assume that I know what I am doing. Once, when I was in high school and touring Washington, D.C., with a group of friends, someone asked me directions to the Smithsonian from the U.S. Capital. I had never been to D.C. in my life and had no idea where I was going, but I pointed them in the direction. I think they ended up somewhere near the National Cathedral. I have been told I have a presence that exudes confidence and shit-togetherness. My wife calls it arrogance.

The four other members of my adopted group naturally turned to me for direction.

Fuck it, let's go right and see what happens, I thought.

"It's definitely right," I announced to the group. "We're supposed to go right."

Off I went with my four lemmings in tow.

We had made it approximately a quarter mile down the trail when we heard someone calling out from behind us.

"Hey! Hey! Stop!"

We collectively turned around to see the septuagenarians had caught up with us. They looked worried and excited. I assumed by their frantic expression and shouts that one or both of them were near death. This was understandable given they were attempting to complete an ultra-marathon in the middle of the desert at their age. Why would a person their age even attempt such an undertaking?

"You're going the wrong way! It's the other way! Turn around!"

Well, shit.

My four new friends turned simultaneously to look at me with a type of disgust on their face I typically see only when I'm naked in the gym's locker room.

They stared at me for a moment or two while I looked back at them innocently, until they simultaneously turned back around and bounded down the trail in the direction from whence we had come. They raced out of sight with the speed and grace of antelopes, joining the spry septuagenarians and Bastard who knew the way, and disappeared from view over the ridge. I was alone in the desert once again.

I continued alone with just the monotony and my thoughts to keep me company: Up, down, up, down, up, down. Right foot, left foot, right foot. I'm going to die. I'm going to die. I'm going to die.

Things began to get direr. The sun rose higher in the sky, and the temperatures rose with it. I ran out of the gooey energy gels that runners are supposed to carry. My CamelBak ran dry. My legs felt ever more leadened. The vultures were circling again.

Then something altogether miraculous occurred. I rounded a ridge, and there in the distance was the finish line. I could see the banner far

off and a group of people that looked like the size of tiny ants. The end
was in sight. But it was still so very far away.

I hunched over and put my hands on my knees. My legs did not feel
movable.

"I can't do this," I whispered.

My spirit and body were broken, and even though I could now see the
end of the course, I didn't care enough to try for it. I was ready for the
vultures and desert to take me like they had Everett Ruess and countless
others before me.

Then my friend motivated me to keep going. Most friends will give you
a pat on the back, but this one was patting my shoe. When I felt the
patting, I stopped staring longingly at the finish line in the distance and
looked down.

An eight-inch-long hairy tarantula had crawled onto my foot.

Suddenly, my adrenaline surged, and my legs felt as light as a vulture's
feather. I flew down the trail with the speed of a cheetah.

Jim was waiting for me at the finish line. He had been there so long
ahead of me that the sweat had dried from his brow and clothes, and he
looked energized and rejuvenated. I instantly hated him.

"You did it! Congratulations!" he yelled with the enthusiasm of one of
those people who lead group fitness classes at the gym.

"Fuck you," I said as I collapsed in the dirt.

"Are you going to be okay?" asked Jim.

"I'll be fine," I said.

I was not being untruthful. As long as I got back to North Carolina and never agreed to exercise with Jim again, I would likely live a long life.

This Is Not a Clothing-Optional Beach

———

I met my wife, Michelle, our freshman year of college. She lived across the hall from my roommate and me and was intrigued by our exceptionally high lofts that we used for our beds.

My roommate had miscalculated when designing the blueprints for the lofts, and somehow we managed to have only eighteen inches of space between the mattress and the ceiling in the dorms. Everyone on the hall stopped by to check them out when we moved in. Not check them out in the "Oh, hey, that's really cool" sense but rather the "Oh, wow, y'all are idiots" and "Bless your heart" sense.

Michelle and I initially hated each other. She was a shy and quiet girl from an upper-middle-class background. I was a loud jackass that made sarcastic comments about everything. Not much has changed through the years. Although we hated each other, we were forced to spend a lot of time together because she began dating my roommate, Patrick.

Michelle would hang out in our dorm room and the living room in our suite-style accommodations almost on a daily basis, so we began to find out that we had a lot in common.

For instance, we both liked similar music, and she grew up going on vacation to Emerald Isle, which was only a half an hour from my hometown and somewhere I grew up going to as well. We had the same taste in movies and television. The mutual hate we had for one another began to thaw ever so slightly.

Eventually, Michelle broke up with Patrick. She and I became a couple a short time later. This would normally be a sign that our friendship was destined to end within a month. My longest romantic relationship prior to Michelle had lasted only about six weeks as I generally had bad luck with women.

As the spring semester wore on, things became more serious between Michelle and me. Michelle told me she wanted to introduce me to her parents close to the end of the semester. This caused me pause and a lot of anxiety because, before then, I had not been able to hold a relationship together long enough to reach this phase. In high school, I had met a girl's family on a date on only one occasion.

The girl, Nicole, and I went to a fancy dinner at the nicest restaurant in my hometown, which is not saying much as its main competition was the Chic-Fil-A or the Bojangles' down the street.

She was excited to be out in the "big city" of New Bern, North Carolina, since she was from a neighboring town called Vanceboro. Vanceboro is essentially just a speed trap where every resident takes the first day of hunting season off work and school. This should have been my first warning sign.

Nicole ordered a Shirley Temple to drink. I suppose she was trying to prove to me, the city boy, that she was refined and had class, even though Jed Clampet would feel right at home in her hometown. She proceeded to place the maraschino cherry garnishing the drink on the white table cloth mere millimeters from the empty bread plate. It's okay, I thought. I can teach her how to do things. Then it came time to order the food.

"What's good here?" Nicole asked.

"The prime rib is pretty good."

"That comes with barbecue sauce, right?"

"Um, it's not that kind of rib."

"Oh. What is it then?"

After an awkward hour of small talk and watching Nicole chew with her mouth open while eating her steak, the dinner was finally over, and the check was paid. It was time to drive her back to her place out in the country.

The drive reminded me of a horror movie scene as the home was down a long dirt road surrounded by forest and not another living soul in sight. We eventually pulled up to a farmhouse that had seen better days.

"Do you want to come in?" asked Nicole.

Of course I wanted to come in. Nicole was very attractive, and my teenage hormones and misguided hope led me to believe that there was only one way this night was going to end. I was going to get laid.

"Yes," I said, trying to hide my eagerness.

We walked up the front steps to the large sprawling front porch of the farmhouse. It took Nicole a while to dig her house keys out from her purse since there was no exterior light, and you could not see any lights from the inside. The moon was the sole illumination, which was both romantic and frightening at the same time given our remote location, Nicole's affinity for hunting, and the fact that really all I knew about her was she had ample cleavage.

We entered the foyer of the home, and Nicole flipped on the hallway light. I was aghast. I had somehow intended to enter a quaint farmhouse but instead had stepped into a Cracker Barrel. Antique garbage littered the walls, and everything was paneled in wood.

"Follow me," Nicole coyly commanded.

We began walking down the hallway toward a backroom instead of upstairs where I presumed her bedroom would be located. We finally reached the family room, and I discovered we were not alone.

An elderly couple was sitting Indian-style on the family room floor in front of an old TV. These, I would come to find out, were Nicole's grandparents. She lived with them since her mother was apparently in prison and her father's whereabouts were unknown.

The grandparents were weaving baskets and preparing to watch a movie. Yes, they were actually weaving baskets. Had I stepped into the eighteen century?

Nicole invited me to sit on a floral print couch beside her, just feet from her grandparents and their half-woven baskets. I realized I could not politely excuse myself at this point, and even worse, I realized that I probably was not going to get laid.

We began watching the movie. The selection of the evening was *Where the Heart Is* starring Natalie Portman. The plot is essentially this: Natalie Portman's boyfriend breaks up with her, and with nowhere else to go, she begins living in a Wal-Mart and eventually gives birth to her now ex-boyfriend's baby in the store one day. It was like I was watching my future with Nicole unfold right before my eyes. Nicole watched the movie laying down, with her head resting in my lap—firmly in my lap at that, as in directly on my crotch area. It would have been awkward had her grandparents been paying us any attention. Those baskets were not going to weave themselves.

I have been told that *Where the Heart Is* is only a two-hour-long movie. Of course, that night, it felt like a four-hour marathon rivaling *Gone with the Wind*. I bet a classy girl like Scarlett knew what prime rib was. I bid Nicole and her grandparents farewell once the movie was finally over. I then drove quickly out of the area and never saw Nicole again.

I was apprehensive about meeting Michelle's parents given my previous experience with the basket-weaving grandparents. Michelle assured me I would not have a repeat of that experience. Her father was an accountant, and her mother was an elementary school teacher. She had a sister who was seven years younger than us.

Her family was the perfect archetype for suburbia: upper-middle-class family with two blonde children, two professionals, a cat, a big house in a neighborhood with similar big houses, and a minivan. They went to church every Sunday and on the major holidays, too. It was the household from *Leave It to Beaver*.

My family was the opposite of hers. I worried whether I could fit in or make a good impression given how I was raised. My parents were middle-class administrative professionals who did not go to a four-year university. I was the only child. We lived in a modest ranch-style home. We never went to church, not even on major holidays like Christmas or Easter. We cussed a lot and tried to avoid other people. It was the household from *All in the Family*.

The first meeting went well despite my anxiety and misgivings. Her father and I had a lot in common and shared many of the same hobbies. He mountain biked, and so did I. He fished, and so did I. He had just bought a new gun and took me to the shooting range to show it off. I showed him a tight cluster on the head of the target in case he got ideas. We developed a mutual respect for each other.

Her mother and I had less in common. She liked to talk about gardening and birds. I did not. She liked to talk about church and was a devout evangelical. I could not remember the last time I had been in church. She loved to play classical piano. I played country music on my iPod. We essentially had nothing in common at all and developed a mutual suspicion of each other.

As the months went by, the relationship between Michelle and me showed no signs of waning. Summer came around, and I was invited to come along for their family vacation in Emerald Isle. I did not see a way I could politely decline while not upsetting Michelle.

Michelle was excited for me to come. Her parents were those cool parents of which most teenagers dream, she claimed. They allowed you to drink underage and even purchased you whatever alcohol you wanted and as much as you wanted. Michelle claimed it would be fun.

I doubted her claims. Learning that her parents contributed to the delinquency of minors only heightened my nervousness about accepting the invitation, not because I was a straitlaced goody two shoes, but because I was quite the opposite. Michelle did not know my history, and neither did her parents. My underage drinking exploits were legendary among my friends and are still talked about to this day. It all began with prom.

My date and I went with a bunch of friends to the beach after prom. We were allowed to stay at my date's parents' beach house in Emerald Isle unsupervised. This was obviously a mistake on their part. An even bigger mistake was purchasing half of a liquor store for our enjoyment that night. It was going to be a good night as far as we were concerned.

I was not big on sharing with others since I was raised an only child. I was also a fairly sheltered child with overly protective parents, and in my youth, I was just itching to rebel and let my wild side loose.

My parents did not drink and constantly warned me not to drink myself because some distant relative long dead was an alcoholic and, therefore, logically I would become an alcoholic as well if I took a swig of whiskey or a sip of beer.

My parents' supposition as to what would occur if I imbibed alcohol was of course misguided and false. I did not become an alcoholic, and this was evident to everyone who had seen me drink at that point in my life. Alcoholics could hold their liquor. I could not.

I became sloppier and sloppier as the night went on. When I tried to walk, I kept stumbling around and slurring my words when I talked. It got to the point where I was not so much slurring as spouting out loud gibberish. My friends tried to hide the remaining liquor from me.

What they did not count on was the talent I had been concealing from them. I am apparently like a search and rescue dog when it comes to finding alcohol. I found the hidden booze in a bathroom's linen closet among the towels without too much effort and in a relatively short amount of time.

I stumbled out of the bathroom and rejoined the party with a bottle of Tequila Rose clutched tightly in my hands. All my friends looked horrified.

No less than six people tried to tackle me and wrestle the bottle of liquor out of my hands all at once.

"You're too drunk!" one shouted.

"Save some for the rest of us," another yelled.

"I'm not drunk. I'm just thirsty!" I kept shouting back in reply.

Eventually, they got the bottle out of my hands and managed to get me into one of the bedrooms despite my protests and diminished capacity to use my legs.

I have no recollection what occurred after I was left in the bedroom. However, I was informed the next morning that I acted like an even bigger idiot once I was asleep.

This, of course, was according only to hearsay, uncorroborated witness testimony, and flimsy circumstantial evidence. The one main rule from the parents was that the guys and the girls must sleep in separate rooms. Another guy who was with us and I wound up in the same guest room.

According to this "friend" who I barely knew, I woke up needing to use the restroom at some point in the night. He then alleged that I stood up fully on the bed itself. To his horror, I then proceeded to strip completely naked. Supposedly, I then relieved myself on the bed. This, of course, was the only evidence presented against me, as I pointed out to my angry friends the next morning.

The bed was saturated. However, I implored, it was just as plausible that this "friend" in a jealous rage poured several bottles of water on the mattress as I was passed out to frame me for a crime that I did not commit. I saw the night before how he was eyeing the bottle of Jack Daniels that I polished off. This was a much more logical explanation than a teenager passed out drunk pissing the bed, I argued.

My friends convicted me anyway. That was the last time my date's parents bought alcohol for us. It was also the last time we were allowed to go to the beach house without parental supervision. My friends were mad and blamed me for ruining their summer plans. I suppose this was fair, if you believed the guy who framed me.

———————————

We quickly substituted our alcohol source and enlisted the older brother of my friend Elizabeth. As an extra bonus, Elizabeth's family also had a beach house on Emerald Isle and parents who placed too much trust in their children. It did not take us long to arrange for a weekend at the beach with plenty of rum and tequila to keep us hydrated.

The sun set across the sound and the moon rose above the ocean around the same time we all woke up from our nap. We ordered pizzas and cranked up the music and then pulled out a deck of cards and threw the beer in a cooler with fresh ice. We would have to wait to drink it since no one thought to chill it before we all fell asleep in the midafternoon.

Several rounds of drinking games ultimately followed. I am generally horrible at drinking games because I can never remember how to play them and ultimately drink more than a medical professional would deem reasonable.

Eventually, I needed some fresh air and excused myself to the upper deck. The upper deck was located just beyond the dining room on the upper floor beyond a sliding glass door.

The sliding glass door was open already to let the cool sea breeze in, so I walked right out. Unfortunately, the door was not completely open when I stumbled on to the deck. The screen door with its black screen blended in perfectly with the night. Some idiot at the party had apparently decided to open the glass door but did not leave the screen door open in an attempt to keep insects out of the home.

I felt an unusual sensation on my face as the screen wrapped around it and heard a loud crack as the screen door ripped off its flimsy track. I stumbled as the door gave way and pitched forward toward the deck railing, which was a mere three stories above the concrete parking area below.

As momentum carried me forward, I managed to catch myself with my hands and push back against the railing of the upper deck. If I had not done so, the railing would have caught me across my hips, and I surely would have somersaulted to my death or permanent disability.

Once my hands pushed back from the deck railing, the momentum carried much faster and in the other direction. Of course, it was difficult enough for me to walk forward, and now I was endeavoring to walk backward. I was unsuccessful and began falling.

Luckily, there was a plastic deck chair to break my fall. A loud crack rang out as the chair refused to hold the weight of my ass when it violently slammed against it. The chair split in two, and I came to a rest splayed on the deck boards. The vibration from the thud my body made against the deck rattled the screen door that had been resting precariously against a plastic deck table. The door dislodged itself and landed on top of me. Everyone laughed.

I awoke the next morning to find the door still on top of me and a plastic deck chair split in half around me. Elizabeth's parents never allowed us to stay at the beach house without them present again, and the brother never agreed to buy us alcohol again. At least not while I was there.

———————

Many of the people in my high school ended up going to the same college. Early in our freshman year, we all got together at a friend's apartment for a party. She had made friends with the neighbors, who were upperclassmen and of legal drinking age.

We made margaritas that night and wanted to be fancy, so we used actual margarita glasses instead of the standard red Solo cups many college students prefer. This was a mistake.

We were all sitting around the apartment talking in a circle and progressed from pitcher to pitcher of margaritas. Eventually, the room was spinning, and my group of friends had magically doubled in size. I was hungry as well.

The snacks were all the way across the apartment living room and in the small kitchen. I didn't have the inclination to get up and stumble all the way to grab some chips or whatever was left. But the hunger kept growing, and the room kept spinning.

I kept thinking about food as I took another sip of my margarita, and somehow my teeth and lips closed around the edge of the glass as I went to remove it from my mouth. *Crack! Crunch!* I had just taken a bite out of the glass.

The discussion in the group stopped suddenly, and everyone turned to look at me. Everyone's eyes, including mine, grew wide with shock as I sat there effectively chewing glass. "You have got to be shitting me!" one of my friends exclaimed.

I realized I had to pee once I had managed to remove the glass from my mouth and pour the remainder of my drink into a Solo cup. Michelle saw me wander toward my friend's bedroom. She had not been dating me long at this point but knew better than to leave me unsupervised.

She was slower than she should have been, though. By the time she found me, I was standing in what I thought was the bathroom but was actually the walk-in closet. I had already managed to douse and ruin about three pairs of shoes.

That was the last party I can remember having at that apartment.

———————

My anxiety increased as I drove over the bridge rising high above Bogue Sound and into the Emerald Isle town limits. I arrived at the rental house a few minutes later and was greeted warmly by Michelle and her family. I placed my bag in my room and went upstairs to join Michelle, her family, and some family friends.

The blender began to whirl, and the sound of grinding ice and slush filled the kitchen as the first batch of margaritas was made. The frosted glasses filled with tequila and lime were passed around to everyone, including Michelle and me and a few other underage college kids who were at the house visiting.

The hours passed, the sun set, and the drinks kept flowing over card games and small talk. Eventually, the adults retired for the evening and left us teenagers to fend for ourselves. This was a mistake on their part.

We grabbed the remaining bottles of liquor and headed out the door bound for the cool sand and roaring sea. We passed around the bottle of rum, each taking swigs of the spiced liquor as we walked down the beach and enjoyed each other's company. The walking eventually turned to stumbling. I'm not entirely sure how, but we ended up back at the beach house rather than passed out drunk in the sand keeping the fiddler crabs and seagulls company.

When I woke up the next morning, my head was predictably foggy, and I was disoriented. I started to open my eyes, but a strange sound was filling the room.

I realized someone was singing as the fog began to clear. It was an odd melody, and as I began to discern the lyrics, I realized it was a gospel song. *Shit,* I thought. *Did I die last night?*

The bed was physically uncomfortable and lumpy. The pillow was hard and firm and had my neck angled in a position that made it stiff and sore to move. I realized I was not on a bed but actually on a couch. I opened my eyes.

I must have passed out on the couch instead of making it to my room. I sat up on the couch and looked around.

The gospel singing was coming from the kitchen across the room. Michelle's mother was cooking something on the stove and singing while she worked. Her back was turned to me.

I stood up. The blanket draped over me fell to the floor, and I felt an unusual breeze. I looked down as I cleared the sleep from my eyes and began to orient myself. The hangover fog immediately cleared, and my heart rate spiked dramatically when I realized the source of the breeze. I was naked.

Around the same time, Michelle's mother began to turn around from the stove to retrieve something from the counter. I immediately flopped back down on the couch and pulled the blanket back over me just in time to pretend to still be asleep when Michelle's mother was facing my direction.

I kept my eyes only slightly open so it still looked like I was asleep and tried to remain calm.

Michelle's mother retrieved whatever she needed from the counter and turned back toward the stove. I began to search the room wildly with my eyes for my clothes. I could not find them.

My panic grew more intense as songs praising Jesus continued to fill the room. At the same time, I was begging the Good Lord to get me out of this situation.

My clothes were on the other side of the living room and bunched together under an arm chair when I finally spotted them. There was no way I would be able to sneak across the room and somehow slip them on without Michelle's mother noticing and an awkward conversation ensuing.

As the a capella gospel concert continued in the kitchen, I prayed for death. It was the only escape I could see from the predicament the rum had placed me in the night before.

As I prayed, an angel entered the room. Michelle looked toward me and began to say good morning but stopped herself when she saw the look of utter panic on my face. I pointed silently across the room and under the chair.

Michelle looked confused at first.

"Clothes," I mouthed silently. She cocked her head slightly, not understanding.

I partially lifted up the blanket so she could grasp what was happening. Her eyes grew wide with surprise over my stupidity.

"Help!" I mouthed silently.

Michelle stood there thinking for a few seconds.

It was at this point I knew I would eventually marry Michelle and that she was "the one." She was presented with several options in this situation. The first was to laugh hysterically and draw attention to my predicament. The second was to shake her head in despair at dating a moron and go back to bed, leaving me to indecently expose myself to her family.

However, she chose neither of those options and instead said, "Good morning, Mom. Can you show me where the towels are so I can take a shower?"

I waited until Michelle and her mother left the room and bolted off the couch. I ran as quickly as I could to the other side of the living room and grabbed my clothes from beneath the chair, pulling my board shorts and T-shirt on. At the same moment, Michelle's mother came back into the room.

"Oh, you're up," she said.

"Good morning," I said, standing in the middle of the room and trying to act casual.

"Did you sleep well?"

"Um, sure. How about you?"

"I did, thank you. Would you like some breakfast? I would have woken you earlier, but it looked like you were in a deep sleep."

"Breakfast sounds great. What are we having?"

"Oh, we didn't have much left in the fridge this morning, I'm afraid. But I did see a little sausage and cinnamon buns."

No Seriously, Have We Been Kidnapped?

We were married two weeks after I graduated law school. Bar examination prep courses were scheduled to begin the week following the wedding, so we decided to wait until after the exam three months away to take our honeymoon. The strategy was to avoid the stress of thinking about the exam while away and to avoid the inevitable debate with classmates over what were the correct answers to the problems on the exam.

We could not just get married and then drive back to our townhome, however. That did not feel right to us, nor did it seem like much fun, so we planned to spend a few days at the beach prior to Michelle returning to work and me beginning my prep classes. The morning following the wedding, we loaded up our car and began the long drive to Atlantic Beach, North Carolina.

The hotel was a towering building directly on the beach. One of those upscale establishments where the floors are marble, the staff is overly friendly, and the miniature bottles of toiletries are brand name.

We crossed the threshold to our suite shortly after checking in and were stunned by the beach view off our balcony. We opened the door to let the sea breeze in and listened to the sound of the waves crashing on the shore. I went to use the bathroom after such a long drive.

A few minutes later, we were both laying on the bed listening to the ocean when a noise caught my attention in the background. It sounded like the waves but was more constant and not rhythmic. I got up to investigate and walked toward the bathroom. The toilet was running. I jiggled the handle, but that did not stop it. I removed the tank lid and looked inside, and everything seemed in order except the tank was not filling. I called the front desk and asked for maintenance to come after explaining the problem.

We had arrived early in the day, and we could tell more and more people were filling the rooms around us as the afternoon wore on by the sound of doors opening and closing down the hallway.

It was getting close to dinner time, and we were preparing to go to a nicer restaurant on the waterfront in neighboring Beaufort. The sounds of the doors grew more frequent as more and more of our hallway neighbors also began departing for dinner.

This was the opportune time for maintenance to arrive to fix the running toilet. There was a loud bang on the door, followed by a man yelling, "Maintenance! I got the plunger for your toilet!"

Michelle and I looked at each other mortified. Did this person really just announce to the entire floor that we stopped up the toilet? When in fact we hadn't? This was a five-star hotel, not a Motel 6.

I opened the door to find a husky balding man staring at me with a plunger held up like a sword in his right hand, ready to do battle. At the same moment, our neighbors across the hall came out to presumably go to a nice romantic dinner by the way they were dressed. The woman's eyes became slightly wider when she saw the maintenance man brandishing a plunger in the hallway, and the man made a slight smirk.

"We don't need a plunger. As I stated when I called, the tank itself is not filling." I made sure to say this loud enough so at least the adjacent rooms would know that we had not broke the toilet.

The maintenance man just shrugged and pushed his way past me into the room. The business end of the plunger passed only inches from my face, and I immediately wanted to scrub my skin off with bleach and a Brillo pad.

We left our room for dinner once the maintenance man fixed our toilet. We decided to dine at one of our favorite restaurants on the main street that overlooks the channel and Shackleford Island where wild horses can sometimes be seen. The weather was perfect, and it was relaxing to watch the boats come and go and the setting sun glistening across the water.

I began to feel strange as we ate our crab dip. My throat was a little itchy, and I felt cold even though the temperature was in the eighties. Michelle was a nurse, so I told her I thought I was sick. She reached across the table and placed the back of her hand on my forehead and told me I was fine.

"No, really," I insisted. "I think I'm getting sick. We should stop for some medicine or something on the way home."

"You're fine," Michelle said with an exacerbated sigh. "Stop worrying about it and ruining dinner with your fake man flu."

We finished dinner and walked along the water front before heading back to the hotel. Once there, we stopped by the hotel bar for a while and had some more to drink. I continued to feel worse and began to feel weak as well. I did not mention it because I knew Michelle would just be dismissive.

We decided to go to bed so we could get an early start to the next day on the beach. I opened the door leading to the balcony, figuring it would be relaxing and nice to listen to the crashing waves below as we fell asleep. Both of us got undressed and laid on the bed. We closed our eyes and listened to the soothing rhythm of the waves as we drifted off to sleep.

I woke up in the middle of an earthquake, and the hotel had collapsed around me. A baby was crying from somewhere underneath the rubble. Or so I thought. In reality, Michelle was violently shaking me awake, and apparently the people next door to us had decided to bring their infant on vacation much to the dismay of everyone on the hallway.

"Wake the hell up!" yelled Michelle.

"What's wrong?" I said, still half asleep.

"You've been gibbering in your sleep and flailing about. I think you've been hallucinating."

"So what?"

"And you're burning up. I need to take your temperature."

Since Michelle was a nurse, she always had basic medical needs like a thermometer in her purse, for reasons that made sense only to her. She forced it under my tongue and waited until the small computer built into the handle beeped and gave her a reading.

"What does it say?" I asked.

Michelle's eyes grew wide, and she hesitated to answer me.

"What does it say?" I asked again.

"Let me take it again. I don't think the reading is right."

She forced the thermometer back under my tongue and waited again. *Beep.* Her eyes grew wide again, and she dropped the thermometer as she ran across the hotel room. She immediately got dressed and grabbed her purse.

"I need to go get you some medicine," she said.

I grabbed the thermometer and read the temperature on the small screen: 104.2.

"Wait...shouldn't I go to the hospital?" I asked as the hotel room door slammed behind Michelle.

Once she was gone, I quickly drifted back to sleep. I was out for an unknown period of time before being startled awake again by Michelle's violent shaking. She held out her hand, and there was a multitude of pills of various colors, shapes, and sizes in her palm.

"Take these. Now," she commanded.

I grabbed the pills from her hand and shoved them in my mouth. Michelle held out a bottle of Gatorade in her other hand, and I washed the pharmaceutical cocktail down.

"Shouldn't I go to the hospital?" I asked again.

"Let's see if this brings your fever down first," Michelle replied.

We sat there in bed waiting for the medicine to kick in. I felt worse than I did several hours before at dinner by this point, which should be obvious since my insides were boiling based on the temperature reading.

I looked over at Michelle after a few minutes, and she had fallen back asleep. I wondered if I should be concerned that my nurse had fallen asleep on the job. Eventually, I drifted off to sleep again despite the wailing of the infant on the other side of my headboard.

A short while later, I was having a sex dream. I was lying in bed, and the soft and gentle hands of a woman were pulling my boxers down. Then they pushed me over to one side. This was weird, I remember thinking in my dream. The dream became a nightmare when I felt something long and hard shoved into my rear.

Beep.

"What in the hell are you doing?" I screamed as I realized I was not dreaming and had a thermometer up my butt.

"I needed to take your temperature again, but I did not want to wake you," explained Michelle.

"So let me get this straight. You thought you could take a rectal temperature reading without waking me up? You really thought that?"

"Well, you seemed really sound asleep and were snoring so loudly, I couldn't hear the baby next door any longer," Michelle replied.

I stared at her in disbelief, feeling violated.

"Your temperature has gone down. It's now only 102.9"

"Only?"

"If it's not down more in the morning, we'll go to an urgent care."

The sun rising over the horizon outside our window woke me a few hours later, and Michelle wasted no time.

"Here, put this under your tongue," Michelle said as she tossed me the thermometer.

"You sanitized this, right?" I asked.

"Sure. Just hurry up. If we have to take you to the doctor, I want to get that over with so I can go to the beach."

The thing that attracted me to Michelle the most was how much of a people person she was.

I reluctantly placed the thermometer under my tongue again and waited. *Beep*. 102.7.

Michelle was already wearing her swimsuit and looked annoyed by the reading.

"Hurry up and get dressed. Let's go get this over with," she said as she pulled on some clothes over her swimsuit.

A short while later, we arrived at an urgent care not far from the hotel. After we filled out the requisite forms, we were seated in a waiting area adorned with pastel pink walls and coastal knickknacks, like shells and pictures of pelicans. We were informed it may be a while before we could be seen. Since we were the only people in the waiting room and it was still early in the morning, I imagined the doctor was probably out surfing or fishing.

Eventually, a nurse led us back to an examination room. I perched myself on the examination table, making the thin paper crinkle as I sat down. Michelle sat in an uncomfortable looking chair in the corner. I wanted to say "I told you so," since she denied I was getting sick the night before at dinner, but I did not want to compound my misery by having to go to the emergency room when she assaulted me.

We waited for what felt like five hours before a young woman wearing bright pink scrubs with cartoon fish on them came in. She introduced herself as the nurse and began taking my vitals. When she went to take my blood pressure, she kept squeezing the pump but the cuff did not tighten around my arm.

The nurse kept squeezing and squeezing and squeezing while the pump made a faint *whoosh* sound each time she did so. I could see Michelle getting more and more irritated in the corner, as if she was the one currently sitting on the exam table. *Whoosh. Whoosh. Whoosh. Whoosh.* The pumping continued incessantly for at least five minutes before Michelle finally lost it.

Launching herself out of the plastic chair, Michelle crossed the small examination room in one step and nudged the nurse gently aside. She twisted a small metal knob on the side of the pump portion of the blood pressure cuff and pumped a few times. The cuff began to tighten around my arm.

"You have to adjust the valve to get it to work," Michelle told the nurse.

"Thank you so much. This is my first time taking blood pressure," said the nurse.

"What do you mean it's your first time?" I asked.

"I'm a student intern. I've never done this before."

"But...like, shouldn't someone be in here supervising you?" I asked.

"Probably," said the student. She wrote down the blood pressure reading from the gauge and left the room again.

I knew then that I would die. I always imagined I would die fairly young, but I figured I would grow middle-aged first and be one of those lawyers who had a heart attack or stroke from the stress of the profession, obesity, and a mild substance abuse problem. That was a respectable way to go.

Now, it appeared as though I would die from mysterious illness before ever having taken the bar exam. If the so-called nurse was left unsupervised and couldn't even work a blood pressure cuff, then there was no way I could trust the doctor to be competent.

I sat there for quite awhile pondering what affliction would end my life. Was it cancer? Was it Ebola? A mysterious infection unknown to modern science? Only time and an autopsy would tell.

Michelle continued to sit in the plastic chair as I debated my fate and was growing more irritated that she was missing the opportunity to work on her tan on the beach.

The doctor finally entered the exam room at approximately the same time I had settled on the plague as a definitive diagnosis for my condition. He was an elderly, bespectacled man with white hair. The doctor looked at the chart the nurse had handed him and furrowed his brow. He mumbled something under his breath while examining the nurse's work.

"I'm sorry to keep you waiting," the doctor announced.

"That's okay," I said. "I imagine you probably have a lot of other patients."

"Not really," said the doctor. "I was out surf fishing this morning and lost track of the time. I didn't even have time to shower before coming in to the office, so please forgive me if I smell faintly of bait fish."

I was for sure going to die.

"What brings you in today?" he asked.

"Well, I felt fine up until dinner last night," I began. "Then my throat started feeling a little scratchy, and then I got a headache, and then I felt just, I don't know, blah, and then she woke me up because I was hallucinating and burning up, and by that time I felt like, yuck, and close to death."

"Hmmmmmm," said the doctor. "Have you felt weak?"

"Not particularly."

"Have you felt any heart palpitations?"

"No, not really."

"You're fine. Probably just a virus. It will just need to run its course."

"Run its course? What does that mean? What kind of virus? Ebola? Plague? Dengue?"

"More like Man Flu," muttered Michelle under her breath.

"I doubt it. Drink plenty of fluids and get some rest," instructed the doctor. He walked out of the examination room without writing me so much as a prescription.

"Come on," commanded Michelle. "I want to get to the beach."

"But I'm dying. We need to go get a second opinion."

"You're going to be dying if you don't come with me back to the hotel because I'm going to kill you. I told you you were fine."

"Fine? You are the one who ran out to get me medicine last night and then made me come here this morning!"

"I said what I said. Let's go."

I had been married less than seventy-two hours at this point, but I knew better than to push too hard. I dismounted from the paper-covered exam table and shuffled along behind Michelle who was already halfway down the hall toward reception. We left and went back to the hotel after paying the approximate equivalent of one monthly payment on the doctor's yacht.

We arrived at the hotel and walked through the grand lobby toward the elevators. I still felt like an Ebola patient while I watched the elevator descend from the upper levels and open slowly in front of me. No one stepped off, and I took a few steps and braced myself against the inner wall and railing, hoping I would not collapse. The doors closed behind me with a soft sound that reminded me of CDC airlock chambers I had seen in movies. I turned to Michelle to ask her again whether I needed a second opinion.

No one was there. I did a 360-degree turn around the elevator to make sure I was not hallucinating again. Michelle was nowhere to be seen.

The elevator reached my floor, and I made my way to our room. Once inside, I walked over to the balcony and looked down the beach so far below. In the distance, I could make out the pattern of Michelle's beach towel and the large sun hat she liked to wear when spending the day on the beach.

I turned and collapsed on the bed. In the moments before I fell asleep, I thought that at least we were getting the bad luck out of our system. The actual honeymoon in St. Lucia in a few months would surely go off without a hitch now.

That may have been the worse hallucination I had all weekend.

———————

Our flight out of Greensboro, North Carolina, was before seven in the morning. Neither of us were morning people, so barely a word was said as we drove from our townhouse to the airport, made our way past security, and meandered through the concourse until we found our gate. We sat in the uncomfortable plastic chairs staring at the walls and daydreaming about margaritas until our flight boarded.

It was a relatively short flight to Miami International Airport where we were scheduled to have a three-hour layover before boarding another flight to St. Lucia. We wandered about the concourses as best we could. The airport was particularly busy, and it appeared everyone in the world had gone on vacation the same week, and inexplicably they all had a layover in Miami at the same time.

We eventually pushed our way through the hordes of stressed out travelers and ate lunch at some airport bar then browsed through the various duty-free shops and ubiquitous bookstores.

I checked a departures terminal, and our flight was listed as on time. I grabbed a Starbucks drink, and we made our way to the gate with forty-five minutes left in our layover.

We chose some seats far in the corner and overlooking the tarmac so we could watch the planes come and go to places all over the world.

It didn't take particularly long for me to start feeling some anxiety. I glanced down at my watch at one point and realized we were only fifteen minutes before our scheduled departure time. However, they had not called the flight to begin boarding. This was unusual.

I walked across the waiting area to the impressively large row of monitors and found our flight on the departure list: ON TIME.

I glanced at my watch. Now we were less than fifteen minutes from departure, and there was no line of people at the gate. I glanced back up at the monitor: ON TIME.

I glanced around to see if anyone else was noticing what I was. Why were we not boarding? As I surveyed the waiting area, no one seemed particularly concerned and were going about their normal business seemingly not having realized we should be walking down the Jetway and into our seats by this point.

I glanced back up at the monitor: CANCELED.

At the same time, a voice came over the loudspeaker and began with, "Attention, passengers." I glanced toward the ticket counter and watched an attractive woman of what appeared to be Puerto Rican descent announce that our flight was canceled and we should see the ticket counter for rebooking and further information.

Almost immediately, a line formed at the ticket counter, stretching across the waiting area. It was impressive the speed with which a few hundred fellow travelers had managed to queue up in line in the blink of an eye.

I glanced back up at the departures monitor and did not see any other flights coming up anytime soon for St. Lucia.

Rather than waste time in line, I walked back across the waiting area to where Michelle was still seated. Her mood had soured, and she was glaring out the window. I offered her encouragement that we would get things sorted out once the line died down.

The constant noise coming from the other side of the waiting area did not help our anxiety. I could hear a lot of raised voices and profanity. Some people just have no patience. What was a few hours' delay until being rebooked on the next flight? We were headed to a Caribbean paradise. Relax.

The line died down, and the waiting area thinned out. I assumed people had gone to the airport bars at this point. I approached the airline employee who had made the announcement that our flight was canceled and who had addressed the complaints and concerns of the other passengers on our flight.

"Hi," I began with a smile. "I was supposed to be on the flight to St. Lucia that got canceled."

"No hablo ingles," responded the woman.

"No, I mean, I'm not upset. I understand things happen. I just want to know when we'll be rebooked. I assume you have one leaving later this evening?"

The woman stared at me with an expression that conveyed sympathy and annoyance all at once.

"Lo siento. No comprende," she responded. "No hablo ingles."

I had taken enough Spanish classes in high school to understand what this woman was telling me but not enough to respond in any intelligible way years later. I could order a beer and say a few choice curse words, and that was the extent of my Spanish proficiency.

I was mad. I knew this woman spoke English. I saw her do it into the intercom when she announced that our flight was canceled. I saw her speaking to at least a hundred other people that were supposed to be on my flight, and the majority of them looked like they could not speak Spanish.

"Look," I began with a more stern tone to my voice, "you and I both know you can speak English."

"No."

"Yes. Don't give me that crap. I saw you make the cancellation announcement and speak to other passengers. I know you speak English. I know you had to deal with a lot of other people, but I was also supposed to be on that flight. I need help."

She kept typing on her keyboard and ignored my presence. Since her attempt to fake not knowing English apparently failed, it appeared as though she would try to ignore me until I went away.

"Hello? Hello?"

Still no acknowledgment.

"Hola! Estoy aqui!"

Still no acknowledgment.

"Escuchen!" I yelled. I did not know if I used this word correctly, but I remembered my Spanish teacher would always yell this loudly at our high-school class when she intended to say, "Listen to me!"

The woman continued to ignore me for a few seconds and then glanced at her watch. She made a flew clicks with the mouse on the computer in front of her and walked away without another word. I stared at her as she disappeared through some discreet door reserved for employees only.

Through the same door appeared another woman only seconds later. She looked much more pleasant. It appeared we had reached shift change, and this woman was just now getting to work.

"Hi!" she began cheerfully. "How can I help you today?"

I explained our situation, and the new gate agent was much more helpful. She spent several minutes clicking the mouse and typing on the keyboard and several more minutes staring at the screen.

"Hmmmmm," she said.

I braced myself for what was about to come.

"It appears the next flight I can get you on doesn't leave until tomorrow morning."

"Tomorrow morning? We're supposed to check in to our resort today. It's our honeymoon. Is that really the earliest flight?"

She stared at the computer screen for several more minutes as if somehow my luck would change. I knew it wouldn't.

"I'm sorry. Tomorrow morning is the earliest flight. There is another flight leaving tonight, but it's already sold out. We will put you in a hotel for the evening and give you vouchers for food. Is that okay? Congratulations, by the way!"

"Do I have a choice?"

She laughed, like this was some kind of joke. "No."

"What about our luggage?"

She searched her computer some more. "It appears it's already been placed in holding for the next flight. We won't be able to retrieve it out of holding, but will change the flight. I'm sorry. It will be on your flight tomorrow and waiting for you at the airport."

"Okay. Whatever. Can I just get the vouchers please?"

She printed the necessary paperwork. "Here you go. Do you need transportation to the hotel?"

What kind of question was that? Did she assume I would walk or hitchhike? "Yes, we will need transportation to the hotel," I said. She handed me more vouchers for a taxi.

I went and found Michelle still in the waiting area and explained the details of our extended layover. She glanced in the direction of the gate agent's desk with a look that appeared to shoot knives from her eyes.

I uncharacteristically attempted to keep a positive outlook on the situation and tried to get Michelle to visualize what would surely be a hotel on South Beach and delicious food prepared by a James Beard–winning chef.

We left the terminal and caught a cab. We admired the beauty of Miami through the back windows of the cab as it traveled through the crowded streets. There were high rises, couture shops, and palm trees as we waited to arrive at our hotel.

The cab took a turn suddenly. There were far more gas stations and corner stores than couture shops on this street. McDonald's and Arby's had replaced the five-star restaurants. The other buildings had their parking lots surrounded by chain-link fences with razor wire along the top perimeter. The people along the streets were wearing grime rather than Gucci.

The taxi driver pulled into a hotel parking lot. It was a franchise of a large budget chain that looked like it had seen better days. Michelle and I exchanged a look. I was wondering whether the windows to the room were bulletproof. I could see from Michelle's face that she wondered why we didn't just sleep in the airport. At least there was security at the airport.

It was dinnertime by the time we arrived at the hotel, and since we had no luggage aside from our carry-ons, we decided to get something to eat before going up to our room. We opted to dine at the hotel's adjoining restaurant rather than risk being a crime statistic by venturing off the property.

The restaurant was predictably Cuban-themed, and the stained paper menu our waitress gave us listed several authentic dishes. I opted for the ropa vieja, and Michelle had a kid's meal of chicken fingers and French fries.

Michelle's chicken died in vain, with its final resting place a white plate covered in a dense mound of soggy fries. I was not convinced my ropa vieja was not actual rope. We quickly tossed a voucher on the table after a few miserable bites and left for the hotel's bar. We filled our stomachs on overpriced mojitos the remainder of the evening.

Michelle and I were not overly confident when we unlocked our room door and entered. When we walked inside, we glanced quickly around the spartan accommodations and hoped we would escape the night without scabies or a bed bug infestation.

We were reassured by a yellow post-it note on the headboard of the bed. "The linens have been freshly cleaned for your arrival," the note said. I had always thought this was a safe assumption to make at any hotel, but apparently I had been wrong my entire life.

The next morning, we took a shuttle back to the airport. We sat in the waiting area at the gate once we cleared security, and I watched the departure monitor with unyielding fixation. I did not look away from it even when the gate agent announced the beginning of the pre-boarding process, fearing that if I glanced away, it would give the universe another chance to screw me and strand me in the Hotel Diablo an additional night.

Our boarding zone was finally announced, and we took our seats. A little under four hours of an uneventful flight later, we touched down at Hewanorra International Airport at the southern tip of St. Lucia. We deplaned and walked a short distance across the tarmac toward the small terminal building, admiring the tropical views in the distance as we walked.

We proceeded to the baggage claim area and waited for the luggage to begin arriving off the plane. We waited, and we waited. Our bags never arrived.

We walked over to the gate agent and explained that our bags never arrived.

"What flight did you just come in on?" asked the agent.

I looked around. There was only one plane on the tarmac, and the airport was the size of a Wal-Mart, if not smaller. What flight did she think we just arrived on?

"We came in from Miami," I said. "The name on the reservation is Banks."

The gate agent began clicking away at her computer, looking puzzled.

"You were supposed to come in last night, correct?" asked the gate agent.

"Yes," I replied.

"I see. Did they give you any details regarding your new flight?"

"Not really. It was a new flight here. I didn't really ask many details."

"Did you know we have two airports on St. Lucia?"

St. Lucia is 238 square miles. That's roughly one-fifth the size of Rhode Island. I wondered how in the hell a country that size could possibly have more than one airport.

"I...I did not know that."

"Mmmmhmmmmm," the gate agent replied. "At what resort are you staying?"

I gave her the name of our resort, and she pulled out a map of the island.

"You are here, at Hewanorra International Airport," she said while pointing with her pen at the southern tip of the island.

"This is your resort, near Pigeon Island and Gros Inslet." She pointed the pen at the very northern tip of the island.

"You were supposed to fly in here, at George FL Charles Airport," the gate agent continued.

I looked where she was pointing on the map at the airport that was only slightly down the coast from our resort. On the opposite side of the island nation.

"Your luggage," the gate agent said, "is here at George FL Charles."

I stared at the map for a minute while I pondered how the Miami gate agent had somehow stranded us at the opposite side of a foreign country.

"What are we supposed to do?" I wondered out loud.

"It's no problem," said the gate agent. "A few people arrived on your flight who are also going to your resort. The resort has a shuttle van that will take you to the property, and I will go and tell them what has occurred and have them swing by George FL Charles so you can retrieve your luggage. Stay here while I go speak to them."

We waited a few minutes, and the gate agent came back.

"Okay," she said. "They are ready for you and have enough seats on the shuttle. Just go out front through those doors. Enjoy your stay in St. Lucia."

"Thank you so much," both Michelle and I said in unison.

We walked out of the small terminal building and into the shining Caribbean sun. In front of us were groupings of people from the world over waiting for taxis and various resort shuttles, holding backpacks

and tote bags and snapping photographs on cameras of I had no idea
what, because we were at the airport.

We sighted the shuttle van bearing the name of our resort and
approached it with excitement. There were two men in Hawaiian shirts
and khaki shorts standing near it. One of them saw us approaching and
met us halfway, stopping us before we reached the shuttle van.

"Are you the Bankses?" he asked.

"Yes," I replied.

"We have been waiting for you since the agent told us what happened.
Welcome to St. Lucia."

"Do we just get on that shuttle over there?" I asked.

"No," came a voice from behind me.

The voice belonged to another man clearly native to the island, who
was wearing black sneakers, black shorts, black shirt, and black
sunglasses with reflective lenses. He got close to Michelle as he walked
up to us and grabbed her carry-on bag.

Both Michelle and I looked at each other with surprise. By that time,
one of the Hawaiian shirt gentlemen was near us as well, and he
relieved me of my carry-on bag while I was looking at Michelle and not
paying attention to him.

Both men turned around and threw the bags into the open trunk of an
older model black luxury sedan that was backed into the parking spot a
few feet away. There were no markings on the car associating it with the
resort.

"Wait, wha—" I began before being interrupted.

"No time. No time. Get in the car," commanded a Hawaiian shirt man as he placed his muscular arm on my shoulder and started guiding me toward the sedan. The man in all black was doing the same with Michelle.

Within seconds, Michelle was in the back seat of the sedan, and I was in the front passenger seat, which in the United States would have been the driver seat.

The man in black hopped in the sedan behind the steering wheel and pulled out of the parking spot. Within seconds, we were speeding along the Micoud Highway away from the airport and out of the town of Vieux Fort.

I began to be enveloped by a sense of panic. The man in black was not saying anything as we sped around a curve in the highway overlooking the sea. I could not see Michelle in the back, but I could sense her anxiety and apprehension as well. Had we just been kidnapped? This was not the plan the gate agent had relayed. I concluded that the gate agent conspired with these criminals to sell Michelle into the sex trade and me to organ harvesters.

To my left out the window, I could still see portions of the airport, and I debated whether I should try to jump out of the car while it was speeding down the highway and run to the presumptive safety of the terminal, or at least out on the runway where I would attract attention and my kidnapping would be stopped.

I then remembered Michelle was in the back seat, and I would not be able to communicate this plan to her without the man in black knowing, effectively leaving her alone to whatever fate awaited us. Since this was our honeymoon, and I had neglected to purchase life insurance for her, I decided against this plan. Chivalry is not dead.

We were now approaching the outskirts of the town, and out my window I could see a structure approaching. It was some kind of stadium, with plain architecture, and at the forefront of the circular complex were the Olympic rings. It was some kind of soccer stadium.

The man in black noticed my interest in the stadium and said, "George Odlum National Stadium." It was the first time he had spoken since kidnapping us.

We continued driving on the Micoud Highway. As I looked through the window, I saw houses, buildings, and resorts buzzing past as we sped along. Soon, the buildings and signs of people grew further and further apart and the vegetation more thick.

We were out of sight of any development and inside a lush rain forest in the island's center a short time later. My anxiety and heart rate only increased. This was the perfect place to hide a body or two, and no one would likely find us in a jungle centrally located on a third world island. The driver began to reduce his speed.

Kidnapping was the only conclusion that could be reasonably deduced at this point. The only remaining question was to what end had we been kidnapped? Was it what I had previously suspected, or was it for ransom?

I decided to try to make conversation with the man in black to ascertain his intentions. I also figured if I could strike up a friendly conversation with him, maybe he would grow to like us and not murder us and dump our bodies in the jungle.

I could now see thick banana trees out my window as far as the eye could see. It appeared to be a plantation of sorts.

"You must eat a lot of fish?" I said.

The man in black glanced over at me. I could tell he was thinking, *What the fuck kind of question is that?* but instead he replied, "I guess so."

"I used to eat a lot of fish when I lived in the Caribbean." Maybe if I could establish with him that I once lived in the same region, we would have kind of a Caribbean "hometown" connection, and he wouldn't want to sell my kidney.

"Where in the Caribbean did you live?" asked our possible murderer.

"Cuba."

"How is it an American lived in Cuba?"

Shit. I had not thought this through. Do I tell him we used to live in Guantanamo Bay and thereby establish a military connection? Would that maybe help and establish that he shouldn't mess with us? Or would it make things worse? Would he panic, murder us, and dump our bodies in the rain forest right now?

"That's a good question," I replied. "Anyway, are these banana trees?" Diversion was better.

The man in black looked at me quizzically again. "Um, yes."

I could feel Michelle giving me an icy glare from the back. I could hear her thinking, *Shut the fuck up,* in my mind. I knew she thought I was only making things worse, so I decided to end my attempt at small talk and think about other ways to get us out of this situation.

The sedan began to slow down even more, and I could see a break in the trees up the narrow and shaded road. As we got closer, I could make out a poorly constructed and maintained wooden building that looked almost like a little shack.

The man in black quickly turned off the road and into the gravel surrounding the shack. He pulled up next to an old analog gas pump. I glanced over at the instrument cluster of the sedan and realized we were almost on empty.

Without saying a word, the man in black exited the sedan and walked across the gravel lot into the shack.

I saw opportunity. "We need to get the hell out of here right now," I announced to Michelle without taking my eyes off the shack.

No response.

"Did you hear me?" I said.

No response.

I turned around, and Michelle was asleep with her head leaning on the window in the back seat. This didn't make sense. How could she sleep at a time like this? Did the man in black somehow drug her?

I was about to try to reach into the back seat and shake Michelle awake when I caught something out of my peripheral vision. I faced fully forward once again, and out the front windshield, I saw several men walking out of the shack, none of whom were the man in black.

One of the men who exited the store wore ratty jean shorts and a plain red T-shirt that had seen better days. The other man was wearing tattered khaki shorts and nothing else. There was something in his hand I couldn't quite see.

Suddenly, he swung his arm out, and steel glinted in the midday sun as it made its journey to its resting place on his shoulder. It was a machete. Both men turned to look at us in the sedan.

We were going to die. The man in black had probably negotiated our sale to these two while he was in the shack. I couldn't make a run for it without Michelle, who was still asleep in the back. It was likely one or both of these men would catch up to me anyway based on their lean and athletic builds.

The man in black emerged from the doorway to the shack and waved toward the other men as he walked back toward the sedan. This was it. This is where the man in black would haul us out of the car, hand us over to these men, and we would never be seen or heard from again.

The man in black walked past my door and toward the rear of the car. He was obviously going to go around and retrieve Michelle first. She would likely not put up a struggle since she was asleep, or drugged.

Instead, the man in black opened the gas cap and began pumping gas. The two men with the machete turned their backs toward the sedan and began walking the opposite direction up the road; their destination unknown. This was an odd development.

The driver's door opened as I continued to watch the two men disappear down the road. The man in black started the engine, and off we went. The man with the machete waved as our car passed them and continued to travel the lonely roadway through the rain forest.

We rode in silence for several more minutes. I glanced over my shoulder, and Michelle was no longer asleep. I expected her to be trying to make eye contact with me so we could come up with a plan to get out of this, but instead she was staring idly out the window at the rain forest. Why was she so calm? Had she resigned herself to death? I thought she was a fighter. She certainly argued with me with vigor and endurance, and I wasn't even trying to kill her.

Eventually, we began to see signs of civilization again. I was relieved because this meant we probably would not be left for dead in the rain forest. Houses began to show up beside the road and so did commercial buildings.

We passed a larger, nondescript cinderblock building that resembled something out of Eastern Europe or North Korea. A fat green cross with legs of equal length adorned the front of the building. A goat was grazing the grass in the yard next to the gravel driveway.

"Is that a church?" I asked.

"Hospital," replied the man in black.

I lost all hope at this point. Even if we were found alive in a ditch somewhere or rescued from wherever the man in black was taking us before we met our ultimate fate, there was no way we would survive if this was the nearest hospital.

I closed my eyes and prayed. I prayed for a swift death and that we would not be tortured. In the alternative, I asked that our captors had lax security so we could somehow escape while we waited for someone to pay the ransom or for the organ harvesters to arrive. I have no idea how long I kept my eyes closed, but I could tell by the twists and turns of the vehicle, it was quite a while.

The car stopped eventually, and I could hear the man in black exit the vehicle. This was it. We were at what would likely prove to be our final destination.

I heard Michelle's door open. I thought it was strange that I didn't hear any sign of a struggle or protest from Michelle.

I heard something odd. "Thank you so much," Michelle said.

Thank you!? Have you gone insane? I thought. I pondered how long it takes for Stockholm syndrome to set it.

A few seconds later, I heard my door open. I opened my eyes, and the man in black was standing beside the door. There was enough space for me to be able to get out of the car and potentially breeze right past him. This was it. This is where I make a run for it. Michelle would have to figure out what to do on her own; it seemed she was already gone anyway by her reaction to being forced out of the car.

I unbuckled my belt and swung my legs out of the car door. I stood up and looked at the man in black, catching my reflection in the mirrored lenses of his sunglasses. My core muscles tightened. My knees bent slightly. My legs braced. I was ready to launch into a sprint for my life.

I turned my head away from the man in black to survey my escape route.

A young woman wearing a Hawaiian shirt was smiling and holding a silver tray with two glasses of champagne on it. Beyond the woman was a pastel-colored entryway with wooden French doors open wide to a grand lobby filled with expensive furniture and a fountain.

We were at the resort!

"Welcome, Mr. and Mrs. Banks! We are so happy to have you here and are so glad you arrived safely," said the woman.

That made two of us.

"We hope you do not mind, but we sent someone else for your luggage at George FL Charles and have it waiting in your room. We had our private chauffeur bring you from the airport so that you could begin your luxury all-inclusive stay with us sooner since you came a day late due to the airline."

Her story seemed plausible. But I was still skeptical.

"I trust the drive was uneventful?" asked the woman.

"Um...yeah, it was great," I said.

"It was great," said Michelle.

Michelle approached the woman in the Hawaiian shirt and took one of
the glasses of champagne and walked toward the lobby.

I looked around to determine whether this was part of some sort of
clever ruse. Glancing around what I could see of the property, I saw
many people who were clearly foreigners to the island dressed in resort
wear and swimsuits and walking around smiling. Only one conclusion
could be drawn at this point: our kidnapper changed his mind.

I approached the man in black, and he seemed to be staring me down
behind his sunglasses as I approached him. I stopped only a foot or so
away from him. Reaching into my pocket, I pulled out my wallet and
withdrew a hundred dollars in twenties. I offered the bills to the man
in black in my outstretched hand.

The man in black took the money from my hand and glanced at it,
ruffling through the bills to see how much I had given him. He raised
his eyebrows.

"What is this?" asked the man in black.

"A thank you," I replied. I figured paying him something in exchange
for not leaving us dead in the rain forest, or selling us to the man with
the machete, was the least that I could do.

"No. No. No," said the man in black. "This is far too much."

What did he mean it was far too much? I understood if he assumed my
life was not worth a hundred bucks, but surely Michelle was worth at
least that.

"It's far too much," he repeated. He removed a twenty dollar bill from the collection and handed the remaining eighty dollars back to me.

"I insist," I said. "It's the least I can do."

"Absolutely not, sir. You must take this," replied the man in black emphatically while offering me my own money in his outstretched hand.

I somewhat reluctantly took my money back. I was grateful the man in black had not killed us or sold us into sex slavery or the organ trade, but I also did not want to be too insistent he keep the entire amount for fear he would become angry and change his mind about our murder.

The man in black gave me a smile once I relieved him of my money and climbed back into his sedan and drove off with a wave.

I turned and walked back to the woman in the Hawaiian shirt and relieved her of the remaining glass of champagne. Walking toward the entrance of the lobby, I could see Michelle was leaning against the threshold and had been watching the final exchange between me and the man in black. I threw back the champagne and swallowed it in one gulp.

"What was all that about?" asked Michelle.

"I tried to give him some money, but he wouldn't take all of it," I replied.

"How much did you try to give him?"

"A hundred bucks."

"You tried to tip him a hundred dollars?" asked Michelle incredulously. "What the hell is wrong with you?"

"Tip him? Tip him for what? I was thanking him for not murdering us."

"Murder? What the hell are you talking about?"

The woman in the Hawaiian shirt was gawking at us. I can only assume she had never witnessed a honeymooning couple begin bickering as soon as they arrived at the resort.

"I'm talking about that man kidnapping us at the airport," I replied. "We were supposed to get on the shuttle here, but two men stopped us and shoved us in that guy's car."

Michelle stared at me with her eyes slightly wide and her mouth open. It was about time she was beginning to understand the predicament we just survived.

"I don't know why I married you. That's the dumbest thing I have ever heard," said Michelle.

Okay, so maybe she was not beginning to understand the predicament we just survived.

"The men who stopped us at the shuttle told us he would take us to the resort. They. Told. Us. That," she continued.

"I...I...I didn't hear that," I stammered.

"That's because you never listen to anyone," hissed Michelle. She stormed off through the lobby toward the reception desk.

The woman in the Hawaiian shirt walked up beside me as I stood there dumbfounded. "Do not worry. She will soon get over her anger. You are in paradise. All couples who have been married awhile fight like this. How long have you been married?"

"Three months," I replied.

"Oh, my," replied the woman in the Hawaiian shirt. "My. My. My. Well, be sure to come here for the honeymoon on your second marriage as well."

The woman in the Hawaiian shirt walked off laughing, leaving me standing alone in the driveway of an all-inclusive couples resort.

The Earth Can Save Itself for All I Care

———

I am not a fan of public transportation. The transportation part is not my problem. It's the public part I find distasteful.

Subways are particularly troublesome. I have no desire to be crammed together with people in a metal tube underground or on a stuffy bus that has to stop every few minutes to drop people off or, worse, pick up more people. I don't even particularly like taxis since occasionally people want to "share" one or the driver is chatty. I prefer to walk or hire a private car.

Several of my friends have preached the benefits of public transportation. It's more cost-effective, they claim. They also tout the environmental benefits. Think of the polar bears, they urge me. Their habitat is melting. While that may be, it is not enough to change my mind on the subject.

My first attempt at public transportation came my senior year of high school on a family trip to New York City. We wanted to get from lower Manhattan where we had just taken a harbor cruise to the Central Park area. My father was with me, and he hails from a small town in Pennsylvania that does not even have a stoplight. Yet due to his training as a United States Marine, he felt he should be in charge during our trip to one of the biggest cities in the world.

We descended the stairway into the bowels of the subway system and arrived at the gates. I was apprehensive about the idea of taking the subway but also slightly excited.

My knowledge of the subway came solely from popular culture at that point in my life. I knew from my childhood that the Teenage Mutant

Ninja Turtles lived in the subway. Had I been younger, I may have still clung to the belief that we might meet them on our journey. I knew better by this point, however.

I had no doubt that rats the size of Splinter existed in this petulant cavern of civilization. Aside from the rats, would we meet alligators? Troll people? Murderous gangs? I concluded all were a possibility.

Of course, we needed a MetroCard first, and we did not have a MetroCard because we were not New Yorkers and had previously taken aboveground, private transportation into the city. A row of electronic kiosks stood along a wall near the gates where we could purchase the necessary cards.

My father approached one of the kiosks and stared at it in a half-awestruck, half-terrified manner. Modern technology taking any form other than a basic personal computer mystified him, as it did with most members of his generation. He, like those before him, came of age and learned to survive in an analog world where electricity was used to keep the lights on and the TV working and for not much else.

I am a millennial, however, possessed with an intuitive knowledge of anything with a microchip processor. I can remember a time before technology, but by and large I, and others of my generation, have a symbiotic relationship with the digital world. I glanced at the kiosk and immediately understood its button and screen. The clear instructions written in plain English on a sign next to the kiosks certainly helped.

Although I was more than confident I could procure our MetroCards from the intimidating machines in less than a few minutes, my father would have none of it. I was still a teenager, so what did I know? He was the adult and in charge of our mission to survive the city of New York. He was not about to delegate such an important task to a kid who spent most of his free time playing computer games. No, Gunnery Sergeant Banks would be in command of this operation and use the computer.

A man appeared beside my father from seemingly out of nowhere. *This is the part where we get mugged,* I thought. The man's skin was grimy, and his hair a matted mess. The T-shirt he wore was no more than a rag and was covered in dirt. His baggy cargo shorts were speckled with holes, and it was clear that his mother's advice to always wear clean underwear was long forgotten. I calculated an 80 percent probability in my head that I was about to watch my father get shanked and robbed of his wallet and watch.

"Hello, sir," said the man politely.

My father turned to face him. "Um, hi."

"Do you need any help? I can show you how to use the machine if you would like."

"That would be great," said my father innocently and without hesitation.

"Ask him what the catch is, Dad," I said.

The man shot me a look. The sort of look I imagine soon-to-be-convicted felons give jailhouse snitches at trial.

"Yeah...um...what is the catch?" inquired my father.

"Well, there is no catch. But if you think I did you a service by helping you out, you could always give me a tip. Making a living in this city ain't easy, you know," said the man.

"Dad, I can work the machine," I said. The man shot me another look.

"No, he can go ahead. I mean, he's the one who lives here and knows how to use it," said my father.

"Great. I'd be happy to. I just need your credit card, sir, so I can pay for the MetroCards," said the man.

My father removed his wallet from his back jeans pocket and withdrew his Visa. In his defense, it had been a while since he had retired from the Marine Corps, so I'm sure his survival training and situational awareness was rusty.

The man inserted the Visa into the card reader on the machine and rapidly pressed a sequence of buttons. A mechanical sound whirred to life in the machine as its printer engaged. Out of the slot came three cards.

The man grabbed the three cards and the Visa.

"We needed only two tickets," my dad said. I recalculated the probability that he would get shanked to 95 percent silently in my head.

"Oh, I know," said the man.

The man threw two of the MetroCards at my dad, and they fell to the ground. My father instinctively looked toward them.

I watched the man run with the speed of an Olympian past us and up the stairway to the street above. He smiled smugly at me as he ran by, clutching my dad's Visa and the extra MetroCard in his hand.

My father was bending over retrieving the two MetroCards when I turned my attention back to him.

"You know, for someone who is working for tips, that was not very courteous," he said while straightening back up.

My father stood there and glanced around, looking bewildered. "Hey, where did he go?"

I rolled my eyes and knew that for the rest of the trip, I'd be warned about the dangers of New York City in between muttered musings about the "son of a bitch" who stole my father's Visa. The good news was we did not have to ride the subway since my father was now of the opinion it was nothing more than a den of thieves.

———————

The next time I traveled to New York was in 2007. Michelle and I were engaged and were making plans to spend the rest of our lives together. These plans included purchasing our wedding bands from Tiffany & Co.

The first day we were in the city, we left our hotel in Hell's Kitchen and walked to Times Square. We then walked north toward Central Park after quickly growing tired of the crowds, neon lights, and billboards. After stopping every few feet to take pictures of the tall buildings we could see around the park trails we strolled—Essex House, Trump Tower, The Plaza Hotel, and so many others—we crossed the street onto Fifth Avenue and began going to the various stores.

We first entered FAO Schwartz where Michelle reenacted the piano scene from *Big*. Next came Barneys, Bloomingdale's, Saks Fifth Avenue, and a host of other retailers. Our load of bags and the merchandise we shoved into my backpack grew heavier along the way. We ended at Tiffany's.

Of course, those of you who have been to New York know that if we were walking out of Central Park to go to these retailers, the logical progression would have been Barneys, Bloomingdale's, and then Tiffany's, as they were closer to Central Park than the other stores. I insisted we do things the hard way, however, because I was not about to walk around Manhattan with a Tiffany Blue box in my backpack. I had watched enough episodes of *Law & Order* while studying in law school to know that if I did, especially since we did not look or act like New Yorkers, there would be a good chance our bodies would be found by a jogger in Central Park the next morning. So I made Michelle walk up and down Fifth Avenue throughout her shopping spree.

By the time we reached the Tiffany & Co. building, we were a sweaty mess since we decided to travel to New York in August. Michelle carried several shopping bags in her hand, and the backpack I was wearing was much heavier than it had been when we began. Sweat stains spread from underneath its straps and my armpits. Our clothes were reasonably priced department store clothes and nothing like we saw Manhattanites wearing. We looked like tourists and smelled like we had just crossed the finish line of the New York City Marathon.

I was apprehensive about going into the store as we stood in front of the building. We both wanted to make our wedding special by getting our bands from this place in particular, and I was afraid that by our appearance we would be laughed at and tossed back out onto the street. The security guard standing at the door in a dark suit, sunglasses, and an earpiece did not help allay my anxiety. I assumed he was security, but by the looks of him, he could have been a member of the Secret Service. I hoped the president wasn't inside to add insult to injury when we were tossed on to the street.

To my relief, the guard allowed us to enter the store, and I was immediately shocked by the crowd of people we encountered. Many of them looked just like we did, and I saw no one who looked like they actually belonged shopping at Tiffany & Co.

Within a few minutes, I realized we had entered the store in the sterling silver department. This is the ground floor where they keep the silver merchandise, which is relatively cheap by Tiffany standards. There is little on this floor that is more than two hundred dollars, and thus it's where the tourists and people who do not have Manhattan penthouses congregate. The salespeople, who undoubtedly worked on commission, looked perturbed and annoyed while they desperately tried to keep the glass cases clean in the war against oily tourist fingerprints.

Michelle and I stood in the center of the hoard and surveyed the room for several minutes. Finally, a salesclerk in a bespoke suit approached us and asked half-heartedly, "Can I help you with something?"

"We're looking for wedding rings," I said.

The dapper salesman gave us a quick judgmental up-and-down look. He seemed to hesitate for a moment, as if he was not sure whether he was allowed to show poor people off the tourist floor.

"Go to those elevators over there," he said, while pointing to the back of the room. "Third floor."

We shoved our way past tourists with cameras slung around their necks, fanny packs around their waists, and backpacks slung over their shoulders. Two sentries were standing guard with earpieces in their ears. I thought for sure they were going to stop us, but they didn't.

The elevator doors opened on the third floor, and there were no other customers. A group of sales associates turned their attention to the opening doors as we stepped off. All of their looks seemed to be urgent; whether it was for a sale or fear that the commoners had escaped the first floor I could not tell.

We timidly began walking closer to the glass cases filled with diamond engagement rings worth more than a year's salary for the average American. Finally, a saleswoman adorned in simple yet elegant jewelry and a black designer dress approached us. "Can I help you with something?"

"We're looking for wedding bands," I said.

"Of course. Right this way."

The saleswoman led us over to a glass case that had rows of wedding bands. Most of them were speckled with diamonds of various shapes and sizes. She began by showing us those, as if she could not tell that they were far out of our price range. This was polite in a sort of way but also a waste of time.

"We're actually just looking for simple bands," said Michelle.

The saleswoman nodded knowingly and pulled some plain wedding bands of various widths out of the case.

Michelle and I studied the bands and selected two that matched what we had in mind. "These are perfect, except, do they come in white gold?" asked Michelle. The bands we had selected were yellow gold, and neither of us were a fan.

I held the ring in my hand and glanced at the price tag. It was more expensive than what we could get somewhere else, but not prohibitively so.

"They do not, unfortunately," said the saleswoman. "The closest we have to white gold in these bands are platinum."

"Okay," I said. There surely could not be much, if any, price difference between the two metals.

"Would you like a chair?" asked the saleswoman.

"No, we're fine," I said.

As it would turn out, there is a considerable price different between gold and platinum. My knees buckled when I caught sight of the price tag on the platinum rings, and I asked the saleswoman to bring a chair after all so I would not faint.

The saleswoman boxed the rings up in the famous blue box with white ribbon. She pressed some buttons on the cash register and asked for my credit card, which I reluctantly handed over. I still swear to this day I could hear an executive with CitiBank laughing hysterically from down the street at the amount of interest they would make over the period of time it would take me to pay off our wedding rings.

I placed the blue box in my backpack, and we left Tiffany & Co. Our plan was to go to the Metropolitan Museum of Art next, and Michelle started walking off to the right back toward Central Park where the museum was about a mile away.

"Whoa," I said. "Hold on. We're going back to the hotel."

"What? Why?"

"Because I want to put these rings in the room safe. We're not walking around Manhattan with these things in my backpack. What if we get robbed?"

"Stop being ridiculous," Michelle said, which happens to be her favorite phrase to say to me. "Nothing is going to happen. The hotel is another mile in the opposite direction."

"We are going to the hotel," I said again.

This was one of the rare arguments I won. We walked to the hotel and dropped off the rings and other merchandise we had collected on our day of shopping then walked back the way we had just come to the museum.

Following the museum, we continued to traverse midtown Manhattan and eventually returned to our hotel for the evening. The next day, we planned to go to Wall Street and Battery Park, which was a walk of about five miles one way.

Michelle was not accustomed to so much walking. She removed her shoes while she was sitting on the bed and complained of how sore her feet were. They looked slightly swollen, and we were both excessively sweaty from walking all day in the August heat.

"We're taking the subway tomorrow," announced Michelle.

"I really prefer to walk. I hate the subway."

"I don't give a shit. I am not walking that far on this trip anymore."

I told Michelle what happened the last time I had attempted to take the subway in New York City, hoping to explain why it was a bad idea and elicit sympathy. My plan did not work.

I am not a religious person, but I prayed while we lay in bed that night that I would not be forced to take the subway. I knew God changing Michelle's mind would be a tall order and almost impossible, even for an entity that created the universe in just six days. However, I held out faith despite my poor track record in going to church.

We slept soundly and did not hear the storm that passed through Manhattan in the night.

The next morning, we walked out of the hotel and realized things seemed different in the city, but we couldn't put our finger on it. I was dreading the day as Michelle had not changed her mind regarding the subway. Her feet still hurt, she insisted, from all the walking.

We walked down the block from our hotel to the subway terminal and began descending the stairs into the depths of Hell. When we got to the gates, we found that the subway was closed. In fact, all of the subways were closed, said a Port Authority officer who was turning people away and back up to the street.

"What do you mean all the subways are closed?" asked Michelle.

"What I said, ma'am. All the subways are closed today."

"Why?" asked Michelle, distraught.

"Ma'am, you didn't hear the storms last night?"

"Storms? No, I was too exhausted and slept through everything. This idiot made me walk everywhere yesterday."

"Yes, ma'am. Storms rolled through last night, and the subways are shut because of it. A tornado hit Brooklyn. First tornado in 118 years to strike Brooklyn. Rains swamped the subways."

Michelle stared blankly at the officer trying to comprehend the fact that a tornado had somehow rolled through Brooklyn.

I thought about how I really needed to be more specific in my prayers next time.

We walked the five miles to the financial district and then toured the sites there. Michelle was practically limping by the time we were done. We ate lunch, and it was time to head back uptown. Subway service had still not been restored.

"Let's take a cab," said Michelle.

"Are you crazy?" I asked. "Cabs are super expensive, and they'll only rip us off because we're from out of town. Plus they smell weird."

Michelle stared at me with that look wives give their husbands when they are in trouble, and we were not even married yet.

"Besides," I continued, "everyone is taking cabs because the subway is shut down. We'll be standing on the curb trying to hail one forever. And then we'll have to share one with God knows who."

The thought of having to stand on her feet for an indefinite period of time hoping for an open cab quickly changed Michelle's mind.

We left the restaurant for lunch, and I thought our debate had ended and we would be walking back uptown. Alas, it was not to be. Suddenly, Michelle walked down the stairs of a subway entrance without announcing her intentions. I stood on the street perplexed.

I was not sure what she was doing as I knew she couldn't get on the subway. Michelle emerged with two MetroCards in her hand.

"What do you plan to do with those?" I asked.

"We're taking the damn bus uptown," she said.

"The bus?" I exclaimed.

"Do you really want to argue with me about this?"

She gave me a look that indicated I did not, in fact, want to argue with her about taking the bus.

We waited at the bus stop only a short time before the Metro bus pulled up to the stop. We boarded and made our way toward the back. Fortunately, there were not that many people on it. It wouldn't take long for our fortunes to change.

With each stop, the bus grew more crowded. The people were of all shapes and sizes, mostly of the large and round varieties. There were a mixture of tourists and native New Yorkers alike, all trying to get to midtown or uptown and all upset that the subways were not working. All except for me, of course.

Eventually, we got up from our seats and decided to stand. Not only were we uncomfortably pressed against the edge of the bench by the other people who had forced their way onto it, but sitting, as it turned out, was not ideal on public transportation. The choice of body odor from armpits exposed while people held the handholds narrowly won out over the stench of peoples' sweaty asses in our faces while seated.

The bus kept loading more and more people. For every four loaded, only one or two would get off. Eventually, the bus became overcrowded, and I was sure there was some kind of safety regulation governing our situation that was being violated.

Sardines had more room in their tin can than we did on that Metro bus. The bus reached full capacity, and I could barely breathe. There was not a square millimeter of my body that was not touching someone else. The smell of sweat and someone's mystery meat lunch from a street vendor filled the compartment. The air was thick with annoyance and anger.

The bus stopped at yet another stop, and we were still only three-fourths of the way to our destination. More people were attempting to get on. I thought about what must have been wrong with them—whether they were mentally infirm or just blind for wanting to get on a bus so crowded.

"This bus isn't moving until you people move back and make more room," announced the bus driver.

By this time, my face was near buried in the armpit of the man beside me, and my left arm that was holding the handhold had gone numb. It was not like we needed to hold the handholds anymore, as we were so tightly packed there was no way any of us would move in the event of an emergency stop or violent crash. If I could have turned my head even a fraction, I was quite sure I would see there was no room for us to move back. Surely, the bus driver had to have seen this in the rearview mirror.

"There's no room to move back," said a woman from somewhere nearby me in a readily identifiable Long Island accent.

"I said this bus ain't moving until you people move back and make more room," the bus driver commanded.

"And she said there is no more room to move back," said another New Yorker.

Mumbled agreement came from the crowd.

There was a period of silence as the bus driver just sat there. I could feel the tension building in the air among our fellow passengers. The August heat and cramped conditions were putting everyone in a noncompliant mood.

"Michelle," I whispered.

"Yes?" came her whispered reply from behind me.

"We have to get off of here. It can't be that much further to walk."

"Okay. Fine. I can't take this anymore," she said.

As we began to try to force our way off the bus, the cordial disagreement between the driver and his passengers turned into a full-out mutiny.

"You better get this fucking bus moving," yelled the Long Island woman.

"I said you need to make room first," said the obstinate bus driver. This man apparently had no concern for his personal safety.

"Get this bus moving now," said another passenger.

"We ain't fucking playing around, motherfucker," said someone with a Brooklyn accent.

The crowd began to swell forward in direct defiance of the bus driver and with the possible intent to commandeer the bus.

Michelle and I pushed our way out through the crowd and the bus's rear door. Standing on the sidewalk in front of a Duane Reade, we glanced back at the bus and saw it rocking slightly. I would have prayed for the well-being of the bus driver, but frankly, whatever was happening on the bus was his fault anyway.

We took a deep breath of New York fresh air, savoring the smell of sweet, half-rotten garbage. It was the smell of freedom.

––––––––––––

Our next journey to New York came a half decade later. Michelle is a huge fan of Christmas, so we planned a trip to the Big Apple in December to see the Christmas sights as her gift. We were going to go ice skating at Rockefeller Center, marvel at the decorated shops along Fifth Avenue, see the Nutcracker Ballet at Lincoln Center, and attend a performance of the Rockettes.

We were also going to ride the subway. This was a nonnegotiable condition of the trip Michelle made before we ever left Raleigh as her feet were still sore, according to her, from the amount of walking we did on the prior trip.

I agreed to ride the subway since I no longer had an aversion to it. By this point, I had been practicing law for four years, so the light of hope within and my will to live had long since been extinguished by the demands of the legal profession. There was nothing the New York City subway could throw at me that would create more anxiety or fear than the demands of constant litigation. Or so I thought.

Our first ride on the subway began uneventfully. It was a workday, and the train was crowded, but everyone seemed to be minding her own business as we made our way from our midtown hotel toward the Flatiron District.

I noticed a man begin to stand from his seat as I was darting glances around the train car looking for suspicious activity. He was wearing faded blue jeans and a tattered sweater and looked like he had had a rough life. He stood at least six foot two and weighed a minimum of 250 muscular pounds.

New York was still less than two months removed from the destructive force of Hurricane Sandy. However, life was going about as life in the city always had. This stranger seemed like he wanted to remind of us of what had happened.

"Excuse me!" began the man. I glanced around, and no one was paying him any attention. "Excuse me!"

He began pacing up and down the subway aisle. "My family and I lost everything in Hurricane Sandy. The roof was blown off our home, and the foundation flooded."

I continued looking around, and some of the other people on the train were beginning to roll their eyes. Others still were trying to concentrate on their phones, newspapers, or books.

"We have nowhere left to go. We've been living on the street—myself, my wife, and my little girl, who is only ten. All of our possessions have been lost. I was wondering..."

"Will you shut up?" asked a bespectacled middle-aged woman sitting directly across from me. She was no more than five feet tall and weighed maybe 110 pounds.

The hurricane victim shot her a glare and continued, undeterred.

"Anyway, like I was saying, we lost everything, and my family and I have been living on the streets since the storm." He continued pacing up and down the subway aisle but seemed to slow his pace each time he walked past me.

The woman across the aisle was trying to concentrate on the book in her hands. I could make out the title from the angle: *How to Win Friends and Influence People* by Stephen Covey.

"My family and I would be incredibly grateful if you could find it in your hearts to help us out with some spare change," continued the man.

He paused. I looked at my watch, wondering how long it would be until our stop, and discreetly glanced around the car and saw that no one was paying the man any attention.

"We could really use whatever you could spare. We've lost everything," said the man again. This time, there seemed to be a sense of urgency growing in his voice.

No one on the train car made a move to reach for his wallet or into her purse.

"No, really, any little..."

"I said, could you *please* shut up?" asked the diminutive woman across from me once again. She was glaring at the man directly and looking him straight in the eyes. "People just want to get where they are going in peace. Shut Up."

To my surprise, the man stood there for a minute or two staring at this small yet feisty lady and stopped panhandling.

I began to feel more relaxed, stopped staring at my feet, and lifted my head up to read the advertisements lining the top of the subway car.

The homeless man began to move again and got closer and closer to me as he made his way down the aisle. He was quiet this time and no longer begging for money. I glanced toward my right in the direction he seemed to be walking and noticed the only empty seats were much farther down the car, so there was no danger he would be sitting anywhere near me.

I turned to face forward again, and the man's crotch was in my face. He had stopped directly in front of me and had turned to face me. There was a noticeably long bulge in his faded and dirty jeans.

"Hey, man," said the homeless man. "Can you spare some change?"

"I...I...I don't have any," I said timidly.

The man began fondling the bulge in his pants. I could now make out that it was a switchblade.

"C'mon, man. I know you must have some money."

I could feel the train decelerating. We were approaching the next stop, a possible escape, but I knew this man would still have plenty of time to cut me with his knife and take my wallet if I didn't hand it over to him voluntarily or think of some other way out of my predicament. Fortunately, I did not have to do either.

"I said shut the fuck up, asshole," the small woman said. Her tone had changed from annoyance to anger. "I am trying to read. Everyone's got problems, and you're no different. You need money? Get a job and go work for it like everyone else."

The homeless man spun around on his heels so his ass was now in my face. "What is your problem, lady? I ain't talking to you!"

The tiny woman was up out of her seat now and was yelling at the man who had at least a foot of height on her, finger jutting into his face.

I looked at the pair in awe and then glanced around the train car to commiserate with the other passengers who also must have been watching this spectacle.

Only not one was watching. Everyone was going about his business as if nothing was happening. What was wrong with these people? Nothing, of course—they were just New Yorkers.

The train had come to a stop, and the argument continued. The doors opened, and although it was not our stop yet, I thought about grabbing Michelle's hand and running off the train. She was playing a game on her phone and looked like she had no interest in escaping the soon-to-be-homicide unfolding directly in front of us.

The woman was really angry at this point, and the man took a step back from her. His ass moved extremely close to my face. I turned my head and prayed this woman did not literally scare the shit out of him.

Suddenly, the man said, "Fuck this," and walked off the train.

The doors closed, and the train got underway again. The tenacious woman returned to her seat and resumed reading *How to Win Friends and Influence People* like nothing had ever happened.

I realized I was staring at her, studying this woman who no one else had seemed to notice and yet had saved us all. The problem was she noticed me looking at her. "What the fuck are you looking at?" she asked me.

I shut my eyes tightly, and I said, "Nothing."

"You're goddamn right nothing."

I did not open my eyes again until Michelle nudged me and told me we had reached our stop.

Later in our trip, we ate dinner at The Stanton Social in the financial district. We had spent the day in the Flatiron District and Greenwich Village so had actually walked the rest of the way.

Michelle was insistent that we take the subway back to the hotel after dinner since it was late at night. She claimed it was for safety, and I was pretty sure she meant mine, should I attempt to make her walk all the way to midtown.

We entered the subway on Essex Street, on the edge of Chinatown and only a few blocks from the restaurant. I was pleasantly surprised when we stepped on to the train car and found most of the train empty. There were perhaps three other people in the entire car, all minding their own business. We found a completely empty bench near the middle and made ourselves comfortable.

The train remained relatively empty at the first stop along the route. The only people to enter the car at the station was an elderly Chinese couple. They shuffled along the car toward our direction as the doors shut behind them and the train began moving.

I turned to say something to Michelle and felt a heavy pressure on my right thigh. The Chinese woman had sat on me. No, not next to me—directly on my lap like I was some sort of young and well-dressed version of Santa Claus.

What was happening? I could not wrap my brain around it. The entire car was empty, yet this elderly woman had chosen to sit directly on me. She said nothing as she sat there. Michelle had taken notice, and she was trying to stifle her laughter.

The woman's husband sat down a foot or two next to us and stared straight ahead as if his wife had not just plopped down on another human being.

The pressure on my thigh from the old woman's ass began to shift. She began to slide down the side of my thigh until she was seated on the bench. Her left leg, hip, and arm were touching the right side of my body.

I glanced at the woman, but she stared straight ahead along with her husband. I stared at the side of her face for a while hoping to get an acknowledgment. Certainly, she must see me. Certainly, she must have felt me. Yet she stared straight ahead refusing to acknowledge me no matter how long and hard I looked at her. Michelle had done this many times when upset with me.

Michelle was laughing to herself now as if this had not been all her fault for making me take the subway to begin with. I looked around the train car, and the few other passengers predictably were not paying us any mind at all.

I faced Michelle and nudged her with my left elbow, tilting my head to communicate that I wanted her to scoot down. She did so, and then I scooted to my left to place some distance between myself and the elderly woman.

A few seconds later, I felt a nudge to my right and the woman's presence against my body again. Inexplicably, she had moved down with us and was pressing against me once more.

"Excuse me," I said.

No response.

"Ma'am?"

No response.

I nudged Michelle again, making her move to the far end of the bench and press herself up against the arm rest to give us even more distance. I followed her and put several more inches between ourselves and the elderly couple.

The elderly woman followed and came to rest against me once more.

The subway was claustrophobia-inducing enough. The stale air, the crowds of people, and the lack of any sunlight always made me feel a little uneasy. So did my prior experiences. Now I was trapped between my wife on one side and this elderly weirdo on the other.

I know what you are thinking. If the train was so empty, why didn't I just move to another bench or stand to escape my predicament? The answer is because chivalry is not dead. What was I supposed to do? Move only to have the Chinese woman sit on top of Michelle? I was much larger than Michelle was so there was less risk of the Chinese woman's weight smothering me.

When the train finally reached our stop, I dislodged myself from between Michelle and the old woman. I turned to face the woman, and she continued to stare blankly ahead. She was almost catatonic. Michelle got up from the bench and followed me off the train.

We climbed the steps up to Lexington Avenue, and I was relieved to be back on the street. Three times I had tried the subway, and three times I struck out. I told Michelle never again would I travel belowground. She rolled her eyes at me.

It took less than twenty-four hours for Michelle to unilaterally rescind my resolution. The next morning, we took the subway to the Financial District.

It's Peaceful Only if You Don't Get Mauled

‎———

A colleague convinced me to go to a three-week intensive training program for trial lawyers in Wyoming. The course was taught on a ranch outside of a small town called Dubois. The town is pronounced "Doo-Boys" because this is America and to hell with the French.

Once I was accepted, I began to learn things about the course that sounded all at once great and horrible. For instance, there was no TV, satellite, Internet, or cell phone service on the ranch. The stated reason for this policy was to encourage us to unplug from the world, our offices, and our lives. We were to focus on the work before us and connecting with each other as human beings. More importantly, we were to connect with ourselves. This sounded fine in a way; I get tired of constantly being bombarded with emails and texts. But at the same time, I am a millennial, and my iPhone is an appendage to my body. How would I survive?

Fortunately, I am a nature lover, and there is no better place to be one than Big Sky Country. I knew I would be okay for the most part once I arrived on the ranch. The sprawling property was situated in a valley on the Wind River Range just south of Shoshone National Forest. A river flowed through it and provided the constant and soothing sound of a running stream. The property was surrounded by mountains. Wildlife like deer and the occasional moose could be seen.

Most lawyers hold seminars in places you would expect lawyers to hold seminars: swanky hotels at the beach, mountains, or some other resort-heavy locale. The ranch we were staying at was not a swanky hotel by any means. Most of our rooms were in a converted old barn.

The doors to the rooms were cheap and flimsy, and my room was on an exterior hallway. I was certain that if a bear, mountain lion, moose, or even a prairie dog wanted to force itself into the room to eat me, it would have to expend little effort in doing so. The bathrooms were also communal, to provide an unpleasant dorm experience first thing in the morning.

Orientation occurred once we arrived at the ranch. We were shown where the mess hall was, shown where our classrooms would be, and given an agenda for our three-week training on how to become better trial lawyers. There was an optional hike every morning as well, which began at sunrise and led to the top of one of the surrounding mountains that could be seen in the distance. No, thanks. I would rather sleep.

The first two days without any connection to the outside world were nice and pleasant. It was like camping back in my childhood before cell phones were readily accessible. It was nice not to be hassled by emails, made more cynical by the national news, or annoyed by Facebook rantings.

By the third day, however, I was entering electronic withdrawal and becoming irritable. What was happening over those mountains? How many email notifications did I have right now? Text messages? Has anyone liked any of my posts on Facebook, or Instagram? These were important questions I needed answered. The unknown made me twitchy.

One morning, I was particularly annoyed because I had captured some great pictures of the peaceful river, and I was unable to make anyone jealous of my trip by posting them all over social media. What good was having all this gorgeous scenery around me if I couldn't digitize it and post it on the Internet?

Then a miracle happened. One of my classmates who had returned from the sunrise hike was looking more peaceful than most of us who did not go on the hike.

"How are you so calm without access to email?" I asked.

"I've been checking my email."

My mouth opened in shock. "How?"

"On the hike. Once you reach the top of the mountain, you can sometimes get a bar of service. Not enough to make a call, but enough to send an email or two, or text."

I immediately pulled my iPhone from my pocket and set an alarm.

The sun was not yet up when my alarm went off the next morning, leading to confusion in my half-asleep state. As a general rule, if the sun is not yet up, that means it is too early for me to get up. I begrudgingly got out of bed and slipped on my hiking clothes, however, for the promise of cellular service.

Fortunately, I discovered that the group that likes to physically exert themselves while on vacation aren't entirely crazy and carpooled to the base of the mountain that we would be hiking up. The sun was up by the time we pulled off the dirt road next to the trailhead, and I got my first full look at what I had committed to climb. It didn't look so bad.

I was wrong, as usual. The mountain looked deceptively sloping, but in fact, the trail switchbacked up and down the mountain steeply. It was a long hill with a gradual grade that seemed to go on forever. My sea-level lungs did not enjoy the walk at high altitude.

I had to get a running start to reach the summit as the last fifty feet was an almost ninety degree incline. When I finally summited, I came to a stop, bent over, and placed my hands on my knees so I could catch my breath. I noticed the others in the group were enjoying the majestic vista all around us once I was able to stand up straight again and breath normally.

I'm sure the views were nice, but I did not have time to look. I knew we would be on the summit for only a short period of time, so I immediately walked away from the group while pulling my iPhone from my pocket. I powered up the phone and watched the Apple icon appear, anxiously waiting to see if I was able to obtain a signal as my classmate had promised I could.

The endless blue sky above us was dotted with white clouds drifting peacefully with a breeze so high we could not feel it. There was a cloud directly overhead at the moment. I looked at my phone and saw no signal bars.

I looked back up at the sky and pleaded with the cloud above under my breath. "Please move. Just please move the hell out of the way."

I watched as the obedient cloud slowly drifted away. I glanced back down at my phone and saw a miracle occur before my eyes: one signal bar appeared. Unfortunately, it was only 3G service.

Immediately, I opened Apple Mail and waited for it to connect to the servers housing my three different email accounts that had not been checked for almost a week. "Checking for Mail..." the app said.

I waited and waited and waited some more. Since I was able to have only 3G service, and a single bar at that, it was taking quite a while to download what I was sure would be hundreds, if not thousands, of emails.

It seemed dimmer all of a sudden. I looked up, and another cloud had moved overhead. Panic began to overtake me. I glanced back down at my phone.

One signal bar. But the service had dropped from 3G to 1x. I held my breath and clutched tightly to hope.

"Checking for Mail..."

I glanced up for a moment at the view in front of me. Rolling hills, mountains, and down in the valley was a line of trees and foliage on either side of the river. It looked like something straight out of an Ansel Adams photograph or a John Wayne movie. I glanced back down.

Zero bars. "Cannot Get Mail."

"Fuck," I muttered.

Frustrated, I shoved my phone back in my pocket and went to the other side of the summit to join the others. They were all talking and looking off into the distance at the views.

I sat down on the ground near the edge of the summit and stared off blankly into the distance for what must have been several minutes.

"What are you thinking about as you look out there?" asked one of the course's instructors who was part of the regular hiking group.

I was thinking about the never-ending emptiness before me. There were miles upon miles upon miles of arid soil, sagebrush and open desert. I was thinking about all the places a cell phone tower could be built. Hell, dozens of cell phone towers could be built. The moose and deer surely wouldn't mind that much.

Remembering that part of the course was to learn to be more introspective and to connect with our true selves and others, I replied to the instructor, "Nothing." This seemed better than telling the truth.

I climbed that mountain the next two days hoping the clouds would cooperate and I could get my technological fix. I had no such luck and gave up. My days of exercise on this working vacation were over, and I resolved to revert to my common-sense habit of sleeping in until at least the sun rose. The course instructors had other ideas.

A few days after my trek up the mountain, the course instructors informed us we would have the following morning off from class. This made me feel excited.

The reason for this morning off was to allow us to get further in touch with ourselves and work on our journey of growing as a person, the instructors announced. *Whatever,* I thought, as long as I got the morning to sleep in and do what I want.

"So tomorrow at sunrise, you will get up," explained the instructor. "And you will not say a word to anyone." This would be easy for me since I was not a morning person and usually did not speak to anyone until at least my third cup of coffee.

"Then you will go somewhere on the ranch or off the property where you can see none of your fellow classmates. We want you to find a quiet spot where you can see no one else, and we want you to sit there and reflect. As you do, ask yourselves two questions: Who am I? And what do I want to do with my life?"

This did not seem like it would appeal to me.

"I don't want you to be worried," continued the instructor. "I promise you there is nothing on this ranch or in the surrounding wilderness that wants to do you harm."

This seemed a bit of a stretch to me since I had seen large animals like moose and bison on the way to the ranch. I also understood that there were mountain lions and grizzlies and other manner of predators in nearby Yellowstone and Grand Teton National Parks. I pondered why a ranch run by trial lawyers would subject itself to such potential liability. Perhaps the dangerous animals all stayed in Yellowstone?

"After you answer those questions, come back to the ranch and eat breakfast. Again, you will not say anything to anyone. Silence. Once breakfast is over, gather in the big barn. Okay? Everyone have a good night."

No, this was not okay. "What kind of hippie nonsense is this?" I mumbled under my breath.

I retired to my dorm room that night and made a plan for the next morning. It was a simple plan that consisted generally of me "forgetting" to set my alarm and just sleeping through the morning. I would be silent while doing so (despite my wife's claims that I snore loudly), so I would technically complete at least part of the assignment. I fell asleep listening to the crickets outside and the gentle burble of the river running through the ranch.

The soothing sounds of nature were not what I woke up to the next morning. There were two former Marines in our class, and our instructors had recruited them to assist in making sure everyone carried out the morning's assignment.

I was jerked out of my deep sleep by the sound of screaming outside my dorm room and an obnoxious metallic noise that I could not quite place.

I got out of bed and looked out the window. The two former Marines were walking up and down the pathway outside our rooms screaming at the top of their lungs while banging aluminum trash can lids together.

"Fine. I'll fucking go on the walk," I said to the dark empty room.

I got dressed and threw on my jacket. Even though it was the middle of July, this was Wyoming, and it was in the forties at night. The cold air was a further assault on my senses. I looked around and saw most of my classmates were beginning to wander slowly and aimlessly around the property like zombies.

I began to search for a place where I could see no one else. This surely would not be hard to do in Wyoming since the entire state had a population equal to Raleigh where I lived. I walked the gravel road off the ranch and banked left, following the road for approximately a half mile.

I saw a trail that seemed to lead from the road down to the thick grove of trees flanking the river. I thought it would be a peaceful place to sit and reflect on what the hell I was doing with my life that led me to be freezing in the middle of Wyoming at 6:30 in the morning.

As I drew closer to the river, the trail thinned and disappeared entirely, giving way to tall grass. I walked through the grass and into the trees until I was standing on the sandy banks of the flowing river. The water was pocked with large river rocks that refused to budge to the water's relentless movement. I leapfrogged a few rocks to the largest in the river and sat down.

Who am I? What do I want to do with my life?

"I am cold and sitting on a rock, alone. I want to go get a cup of coffee," I told the river.

I stared blankly at the river rushing all around me for several minutes as I tried to shake the sleep from my brain and wake up without my fix of caffeine.

Eventually, I began to feel more awake and started to look around. To my right beyond the thin strand of trees and foliage was a rocky, dusty bluff that rose for a couple of hundred feet from the river bank. To my left was the tall grass, strand of trees, and sandy river bank, which I had crossed not long ago.

I noticed an indention in the sand and focused my attention on it. It was roughly the circumference of a soccer ball and somewhat deep, as if a person had pushed the ball firmly into the sand.

That's odd, I thought. I had not seen anyone on the ranch with a soccer ball. Frankly, I did not know when they would have the time to come down here to play anyway or, for that matter, why they would be playing near the river. I doubted any of the locals would have made the impression. Wyomingites I imagined were not really soccer people. They were more "let's go ride a bull" or "let's shoot some shit" people.

The more I contemplated the source of the circular dent, the more I realized it wasn't quite in the shape of a soccer ball despite it being round and roughly the same size. For one thing, there were smaller golf-ball sized circular indentations lining one side of it.

No, not golf balls, I realized as I studied them closer. More like cake pops because there was a straight, thin indentation coming from each one. Why on earth would anyone shove cake pops into the sand? Where did one even procure a cake pop here? I had not seen a Starbucks since my layover in Minneapolis on the way to Jackson.

I stared at the strange arrangement some more. Suddenly, the decaffeinated fog surrounding by brain lifted, and something clicked.

I bolted to my feet and stood ridged on the river rock.

OH MY GOD! I thought. I was staring at the paw print of a grizzly bear, and a large one by the looks of it. It appeared fresh, which was the worst part of all. Or I assumed it did. What the hell did I actually know about animal tracks?

I glanced around nervously, still standing on the rock, hoping not to see the beast. Fortunately, I appeared to be in the clear...for now, anyway. I took a deep breath and tried to slow my pulse and remain calm.

Prior to my trip, I knew that encountering a bear could be a possibility. I was actually prepared for this moment since I had Googled prior to coming out to Wyoming what I should do if I encountered a grizzly in the wild.

"Pray." This was the only instruction from the Internet I could remember in the moment.

"I promise you there is nothing on this ranch or in the surrounding wilderness that wants to do you harm." That is what the instructor had said, was it not? What a liar. As a lawyer, I should have known better than to trust another lawyer.

After a few minutes, I began to recall more and more of the post I had read about how to survive a grizzly attack as my pulse slowed.

"Do not run," it had said. Okay. Rather than bolting straight back to the ranch, I decided I would stay on the rock until I could figure out a more logical way of getting out of my predicament. Surely, the bear had to have been miles from here anyway, right?

There was suddenly a rustling in the grass to my left. Until that moment, I had never fully understood what people meant when they said they almost shit themselves in response to something frightening.

A small bird flew out of the tall grass. The moving blades became still.

"Don't scream or yell," the posting on grizzlies had said. That ruled out yelling for help.

"Curl up into a ball." This seemed like a ludicrous idea, but it is what the Internet had suggested. I wished I could remember whether this was something I was supposed to do if encountering a bear or whether it was an instruction for what to do if the bear charged and attacked. I sat back down, pulled my knees to my chest, and wrapped my arms around them.

I focused on the flowing water of the river and began to calm down some more. Then something made a splashing sound behind me. I stopped breathing and shut my eyes tight, preparing myself for mauling.

There was no sensation of claws or teeth ripping into me, and there was no more splashing. I worked up the nerve to glance behind me: nothing. Whatever it was had gone; probably a fish grabbing a bug off the surface.

After a long period of silence, I tried to refocus on the morning's assignment to take my mind off my situation. Who am I? What do I want to do with my life?

These were difficult questions to answer, especially under the circumstances. I thought of several possible answers.

"I am a man sitting on a rock. I want to leave and return to civilization."

"I am a man who needs coffee and more sleep. I want to go get coffee and more sleep."

Thoughts of the Internet article kept intruding. "While in bear country, be aware that you may encounter a bear at any time," it said.

"I am a trial lawyer, smart enough to get out of this. I want to get out of here."

"Try not to panic; remain as quiet as possible until the attack ends," the Internet said.

"I am a man who is going to be mauled. I want to not become bear poop."

"Be sure the bear has left the area before getting up to seek help," the Internet advised.

The clack of rocks falling down the side of the bluff to my right interrupted my thoughts.

My heart jumped into my throat as my legs bolted me upright. I looked around wildly for the source of the rocks falling but saw nothing. I scanned the bluff and saw nothing again. Surely, a bear big enough to leave a paw print the size of a soccer ball in the sand would not be able to camouflage itself and hunt in stealth. That was more of a mountain lion's *modus operandi*.

"Wait, doesn't Wyoming also have mountain lions?" I whispered to myself.

Enough was enough. It was time to leave; to hell with the advice from the Internet. I jumped off the rock and landed on the riverbank with one foot in the bear track and one foot next to it. I ran through the high grass and up the trail that led to the dirt road and back to the ranch.

Once on the road, I felt like something was following me. I had already read on the Internet at some point that if something was chasing you, it was best not to turn around and try to look at it, but rather to keep focus forward and keep running. Or at least I thought I remembered reading that; I could have been making it up in the moment.

I continued running, sprinting really, until I could see the gated entryway of the ranch with its big wooden archway. I turned my head to the right to see what had been chasing me down the road as I turned into the driveway. I expected to see a grizzly the size of a small SUV, or perhaps a mountain lion.

I saw a prairie dog instead. I stopped running and looked at the rodent, which diverted from the road and into a field before it reached me.

I was finally safe.

"That was a close one," I said to myself, catching my breath.

Breakfast was quick and silent in the mess hall as we were still not allowed to talk. We gathered in the big barn that served as our main classroom once everyone was finished eating. The lead instructor had us all sit in a circle, and he stood in the center.

"Okay. So I hope you all had a wonderful time this morning and accomplished a lot of self-reflection," began the instructor. "What we're going to do now is each of us is going to stand in the center of the circle and share our answers to the questions we asked. Who are you? What do you want to do with your life?"

I rolled my eyes.

"Afterward," the instructor continued, "we are going to paint. It doesn't matter if you're a good artist or not. We don't want to see any landscapes. We want you to paint whatever comes to your heart. Your heart, not your mind. Paint your feelings."

Maybe being mauled to death on the banks of the river by a bear would not have been that bad after all, I thought.

The Canadian Hostage Crisis

———

The prospect of returning to the United States following a week in the picturesque Vancouver suburb of Deep Cove was unpalatable. I'm sure it had more to do with the scenic hiking and whale watching than the fact that the 2016 election cycle was already gearing up, even though in August 2015, the election was still more than a year away.

Our choice of candidates already seemed to be either Hillary Clinton or any of twelve Republican candidates who were equally unimpressive and nauseating. It certainly didn't help that Donald Trump had announced his candidacy only a little more than a month before our trip. He was not immediately laughed off the campaign trail, and the media seemed obsessed with him, giving me a bad feeling in the pit of my stomach. We naturally began looking at real estate and Canadian immigration laws "just in case."

We spent an evening in our rented studio apartment gazing out at the water of Deep Cove and perusing real estate listings. It was difficult for us to find a suitable property in Vancouver, or at least in the desirable neighborhoods. Most of the homes were out of our price range, given that we had no employment in Canada and a mortgage back in North Carolina. There were a few that I found that would have been perfect, but Michelle vetoed them unreasonably.

I tried to convince her how perfect a hunting cabin on an island would be—remote, no neighbors, and beautiful views.

"We don't own a boat," she protested.

I informed her we could easily purchase one, or at least a kayak.

"It doesn't have any indoor plumbing," she complained.

There was no satisfying her.

The day came when our Airbnb rental was up, and we had to fly back to the United States. Since I was driving the rental car, we arrived four hours before the flight to allow time for returning the car, printing our boarding passes, checking our luggage, and getting through security.

With the remaining three and a half hours, we browsed the shops and restaurants at the airport hawking poutine and maple-flavored everything.

We were thirty minutes away from our departure time when our flight was delayed. An announcement over the public address system informed us that our flight would be delayed at least two hours due to a "minor" mechanical issue. I never understood in all my years of flying how a minor mechanical issue could delay a flight. A turn signal burning out on my car is a minor mechanical issue. It doesn't mean that I cannot drive it.

During the two additional hours perusing maple-flavored products throughout the airport, I did the math in my head and realized we would have approximately fifteen minutes to make our connecting flight from Toronto to Raleigh-Durham. Certainly this was not ideal, but it was doable with a quick step and determination.

The time for boarding finally came, and we sat ourselves in our assigned seats and awaited takeoff. The plane pulled away from the gate and made its way toward the runway. We taxied slowly and then suddenly stopped. When a few moments went by without us moving again, I leaned over my aisle seat and looked out the window to find we were in a long line of planes waiting to take off.

Minutes passed, and then more minutes. A half an hour went by. I kept glancing at my watch every few seconds recognizing the inevitable but not wanting to face it, hoping against reason that we would take off soon to enable us to make our connecting flight out of Toronto and into Raleigh.

We were airborne an hour after we pulled away from the gate. Once we were at cruising altitude, the flight attendant made an announcement, informing us of what we already knew: most of the passengers on the plane were going to miss their connections, including us. We were told that we would need to check with the gate agent on arrival in Toronto to be booked on a new flight to our final destination.

I glanced at Michelle. "So we get into Raleigh a little later than we originally expected. No big deal."

She nodded and went back to reading her romance novel.

The jouncing of the plane connecting with the tarmac shook me awake from my nap. We had finally arrived in Toronto.

The plane made its way to the gate and was parked. The Fasten Seatbelt sign went off, and immediately everyone in the aisle seats sprang up and began grabbing their carry-ons from the overhead bins, including me.

We who fly frequently knew what was about to happen and what needed to be done. With a plane half-full of passengers who had missed connections, we were about to engage in an Olympic sprint down the Jetway to the gate agent desk. It was important to medal and take a place on the podium to secure the next flight to wherever one was going.

The cabin door opened, and we all began to exit orderly. Once out of the plane's fuselage, no one ran, but we all engaged in a queer type of power walking. I managed to be the fifth in line at the gate agent desk, which allowed me to get my hopes up. I should know better by now.

"Hi there, how can I help you?" asked the perky gate agent as if she didn't already know what would be needed.

"Our plane was delayed from Vancouver, and we missed our connection to Raleigh-Durham. I need to be rebooked."

"Oh, I see. I'm very sorry about that. Let me see what I can do."

The gate agent began typing on her keyboard and clicking her mouse. Her brow furrowed more and more as the minutes went by.

"Okay. You and your wife are all booked on the next available flight to Raleigh-Durham, sir!"

"That's great," I said. I glanced over at Michelle who was in the waiting area and nodded toward her to let her know the mission had been accomplished. "So when does it leave?"

"Three days from now, sir."

"Three days?" I exclaimed.

"Oh, yes, sir. Is that all right? All the other flights are booked."

"No, it's not all right. We're supposed to be home today. Are there really no other flights?"

"No, sir. That's the first available. I am so sorry. Will you need a place to stay?"

I stared at the agent blankly for a few moments. "Of course, we'll need a place to stay. We're stranded in Toronto."

"Oh, okay, then. That's not a problem."

The agent began typing on her keyboard again and handed me ticket-sized pieces of paper.

"These are vouchers for your hotel and meals while you stay with us here in Toronto. There's a shuttle outside that will take you to the hotel."

"What about our luggage? We have nothing to wear and no toiletries for the next three days."

"You can pick up your luggage at the baggage claim desk. That's no problem at all."

I mustered a polite yet insincere thanks and walked away from the gate desk, dazed at the prospect of being held in Canada for the next three days against my will.

I glanced up at Michelle who knew from looking at me that something was wrong. I walked up to her and filled her in on what I learned.

"Three days?" she yelled.

We made our way to the baggage claim area, which resembled what I imagine purgatory looks like. There was a line at least forty people deep at the baggage claim desk. We took our positions at the end of the line.

It was almost two hours before we finally reached the desk. The sun had long set, and we were starving since the only thing we had eaten since the morning was a complimentary bag of peanuts and a four-ounce plastic cup filled mostly with ice and a small amount of water.

I explained our situation to the polite agent behind the desk and asked if we could please get our luggage.

"Oh, no, sir. I'm terribly sorry for the inconvenience, but all our crew back there has gone home for the night."

"I don't understand," I said.

"There's no one in the back to retrieve your bag, sir. Everyone went home. I'm so sorry for the inconvenience."

"I understand everyone went home. I was supposed to go home today, too, but then got stranded in Canada for three extra days. I was told we would be able to retrieve our luggage."

"No, sir. It is not possible."

"Can you not go back there and retrieve it?"

"No, sir. I am not permitted."

"But you are a baggage agent at the baggage claim desk. How is it that you are not permitted to retrieve baggage?"

"Those are the rules, sir. But here, I can offer these toiletry bags filled with travel toiletries for tonight," she said.

The agent shoved the bag toward me with a polite smile.

"You are welcome to come back in the morning if you like and retrieve your bags for the duration of your stay with us in Toronto. They'll be here waiting for you," said the agent.

"Duration of our stay in Toronto." Everyone with the airline so far had made it sound like we had chosen Pearson Airport as our vacation spot.

Michelle and I made our way outside and found the shuttle. It was almost 10:30 at night, and we were eager to get to the hotel and get some dinner and several drinks at the restaurant the gate agent had mentioned was open late.

The shuttle driver pulled away from the airport and began the drive to the hotel once it was confirmed everyone stranded was aboard. The bus was crowded to capacity with our fellow passengers whose trip to Canada had likewise been involuntarily extended by the airline.

We arrived at the hotel at approximately 10:45 that night. It was what I expected from an airline: a nondescript budget chain with beige stucco walls and neon signs. The hotel was located not terribly far from the airport and in an industrial section of town.

The driver of the bus came to a stop in the porte cochère, and there was a sense of collective relaxation on the bus. We may have been trapped in Canada, but at least we were now at a place where we could eat and sleep after a long day.

The relief was fleeting.

"The restaurant closes at 11:00," announced the shuttle driver.

Eyes darted about the bus nervously as everyone now saw their fellow passengers as the enemy in a race against time.

Divide and conquer was our strategy. Michelle would go to the restaurant just off the hotel's lobby, while I would go to the front desk to check in and obtain our keys hoping to avoid having to wait in yet another line when the fellow passengers wanted to check in after eating.

The departure from the bus was fairly orderly, as was the short walk into the expansive lobby. I turned my attention to the front desk and began walking toward it, glancing over my shoulder as I went. Michelle looked like Simba in Disney's *The Lion King* during the water buffalo stampede that killed Mufasa.

I joined Michelle in the restaurant once I had procured our room key. She was sharing a table with an older couple as there were too many people in the small restaurant to accommodate everyone at tables of their own.

We enjoyed our mediocre dinner in the company of these complete strangers, having bonded over our new found hatred of the airline. When we weren't disparaging the airline, we were busy staring at the wait staff fluttering between the tables looking bewildered and confused as their shift was involuntarily extended by perhaps the busiest dinner service they had ever seen, let alone this late at night.

Our room was nice, I suppose, at least in the sense that it was habitable, and we were not sleeping on the airport floor. The view in the expansive window was of the parking deck. The water temperature choices in the shower were either Arctic or Lava of Mordor. Our television allowed for the viewing of *Friends* on three separate channels, a shopping network in French, or for some reason a digitalized aquarium screensaver.

I allowed myself a few minutes to lay on the bed and relax after the long day. Then my mind went to work. There was no way we could stay in Canada three additional days, particularly without any luggage. Our responsibilities at work could wait no more. The dogs needed to be picked up from boarding. We were tired of being surrounded by polite Canadian people and needed to be back home where people honk and cuss at you for any minor transgression on your commute to work. We needed to make an escape, but how?

I picked up the phone and dialed the airline's 800 number. My hope was that someone on the phone would have greater access to additional flights than the gate agent who was bombarded by half a plane full of angry passengers, or perhaps someone on an earlier flight to Raleigh had canceled or rebooked to another day.

I finally reached a peppy Canadian representative after more than two hours of listening to a robot tell me how much the airline cared about me and how important my call was.

"Good evening and thank you for calling Air Canada! How may I help you tonight?" asked the representative.

"You are holding me and my wife against our will in Toronto," I said. "You can help me by letting us go home."

"Oh, my. I am so very sorry about that. Do you have your reservation number so I can look and see what's going on?"

I provided her with the number that defined my existence to the airline.

I could hear the clicking of a keyboard on the other end of the line.

"I see we have you rebooked on another flight to Raleigh-Durham in three days, sir," said the agent after a few minutes of typing. "Would you like to check the status of that flight?"

"What? No, I don't want a status. I want to change my flight. I want to leave this country and go home. Is there not an earlier flight you can get me on? It's not my fault you had mechanical trouble."

"I am so very sorry about that, by the way," replied the agent.

A few more minutes of typing passed. "No, I'm sorry, sir, all the other flights are booked. The soonest we can let you leave is in three days."

"Is there a standby list you can place us on?"

"Oh, I'm so very sorry, sir, but the standby lists are also filled."

A pause.

"Is there anything else I can help you with?" asked the agent.

"No."

"Well, we do very much appreciate y—"

I hung up.

I turned my attention away from the small and cheap hotel desk toward the bed to let Michelle know I struck out again on an earlier flight. She was asleep and seemed content about staying in Canada a while longer.

I stood up from the desk chair and walked toward the thick plate glass window that overlooked some sort of warehouse facility beyond the parking deck. Just beyond the structure was a billboard lit up in bright contrast against the night sky. It read: Enterprise.

I called the 800 number, and after an impossible time on hold for as early in the morning as it was, I reached a live person and explained my plight. Yes, my wife and I were being held hostage in Canada. Yes, we are prisoners in a cheap hotel. The food is awful and scarce. I need assistance in getting us back to the United States.

"I want to a rent a car to go to Raleigh."

"That is too far for a rental car, sir," replied the agent.

"What do you mean? There are gas stations along the way. I am sure of this. I do not want some bullshit hippie electric car."

"No, sir. That's not what I mean. You cannot rent a car if your trip is greater than six hundred miles."

"Washington is about that far from here. Get me another rental car booked there, and I'll switch out."

"Let me see what is available, sir."

I once again listened to the sound of someone typing on a keyboard for minutes of my life I'll never get back.

"Sir, I'm sorry, but it does not appear there are any rental cars available in your area."

"You mean to tell me there is not a single car available in all of Toronto?"

"Yes, sir."

"I will take anything. I will take a minivan if necessary. But only if necessary."

"I'm sorry, sir. Everything is booked. There is some kind of convention that has depleted our stock. Besides, sir. Did you say you were intending to travel from Toronto to the United States?"

"Yes."

"Toronto, in Ontario, Canada?"

"Is there another?"

"Ah, I'm not sure, sir. However, you are not allowed to take a rental car across an international border."

"I feel this could have been explained at the outset of the call thirty minutes ago."

"Yes, probably. I do apologize, sir. Is there anything else I can help you with tonight?"

"You have not helped me with anything tonight."

I hung up the phone.

I began pacing the room, glancing periodically at Michelle sleeping. The airline couldn't, or rather wouldn't, put us on another flight until three days from then and the attempt to leave by car was a dead end.

Michelle would veto any idea that was more drastic like taking a train or hitchhiking.

I sat down and pulled out my wallet to see how much cash we had remaining so I could get something to eat from the hotel vending machine down the hallway. I began flipping through the Canadian currency and thought how odd it was that Queen Elizabeth was on the twenty dollar bill.

Queen Elizabeth. That was it. That was the solution. The Queen City. Charlotte was only a few hours from Raleigh, and we should have no problem getting a rental car at the airport once we landed.

I picked up the phone and called the airline again.

"Good morning, how can I help you today?"

Once more, I explained our plight.

"Can you book us onto a flight to Charlotte sooner than three days from now?" I asked.

There was more typing on the phone.

"Oh, yes, sir. There appears to be a flight to Charlotte leaving tomorrow morning."

"Great. Put us on that flight."

More typing.

"Okay, sir, you are all booked on the flight to Charlotte." We were going home.

I awoke after what amounted to merely a long nap and attempted to make coffee. I groggily filled the pot with water and placed the stale grounds into the basket. When I attempted to turn it on, however, there was no power button. There was a gaping hole where the button used to be, broken off at some point in the past by some sadist hell bent of ruining the lives of others. So there I was, still stranded in a foreign country, running on empty, and without a way to deliver life-giving caffeine into my system.

We arrived back at the airport for our morning flight to Charlotte decaffeinated. I was not optimistic upon our arrival.

I walked up to the gate agent desk after obtaining a black coffee with a few shots of espresso thrown in for extra measure. I was reassured by the gate agent that our luggage would meet us in Charlotte when our plane landed after a few minutes of explanation.

I walked back toward the lounge where Michelle was situated and glanced at the departure terminal. We were still listed as on time, but of course the departure was not scheduled for another two hours. A lot could happen in that time, as often does when traveling.

Killing time is difficult in an airport. The options are to read, people watch, or walk up and down the concourse browsing whatever shops happen to be there. I chose the latter and once again marveled at how many different things could be flavored with maple.

Don't get me wrong, not every shop sold maple syrup of different varieties. There were also the ubiquitous bookstores with T-shirts with maple leaves adorning them and a suit shop. I have long wondered who these people are, the people who buy a brand-new suit in an airport.

The departure monitor now told me what I already suspected upon arrival: Delayed. Only this time it was displayed in French, which fittingly is translated to "en retard." Retarded was the perfect way to describe this entire experience.

I gave up at that point. I bought yet another coffee with espresso added and sat myself beside Michelle who was reading her romance novel once again. The new departure time was scheduled for an additional hour, and I spent the time staring blankly out of the window watching planes come and go. Planes filled with lucky people who were going places in their lives.

We were airborne and en route to the United States, eventually. Perhaps not to home, but Charlotte was close enough. I settled into the seat and began napping until it was time for the flight attendant to make the rounds with drink and food orders.

"Yes, I'd like a beer and the pepperoni pizza," I told the attendant when he offered to take my order.

"Oh, I'm so sorry, sir. We are out of pizza," he responded.

Of course they were out of pizza.

"What do you have?" I asked.

"We have the cheese and cracker platter left, sir."

I handed the attendant my credit card and watched with irritation as I paid ten dollars for six cubes of cheese and five stale crackers.

A commotion arose behind us halfway through my purported meal. Muffled voices could be heard coming from the seats directly behind us, and the ding of the call light summoned a flight attendant.

"Yes, can I help you?" asked the attendant.

"I...I can't breathe," replied a panicked woman.

"I think she might be having a panic attack," replied the woman's male companion.

"Okay, just remain calm," reassured the flight attendant.

"This is her first time flying," said the man.

"Just keep calm. Take some deep breaths. Would you like some water?" offered the attendant.

The woman replied with nothing save for the sounds of hyperventilation.

The attendant walked back up the aisle and began consulting with his colleagues in hushed whispers.

This was clearly a job for Michelle. She is a compassionate person who chose to help people by becoming a nurse. She was used to handling these situations and medical emergencies. I, on the other hand, was deficient in compassion and generally useless in a medical emergency.

I could sense the attendants were debating whether to have the pilot make an emergency landing somewhere other than Charlotte. This would be disastrous for my plans to get home—not only would we be faced with more delays, but we may end up stuck somewhere even worse than Toronto, such as New Jersey or Ohio. I shuddered at the thought.

I turned to Michelle. "You need to intervene and help this woman get her shit together."

Michelle glanced over her shoulder through the small gap in the seat.

"She'll be fine," Michelle said.

"I don't think she knows that."

"Well, she will be."

"I don't think the flight attendants know that either. They look like they are debating whether to divert and make an emergency landing. You have to intervene and help this woman get her shit together. Do your nurse thing. Backhand her across the face and tell her to pull herself together, or do whatever one does to stop someone's panic attack."

"You're being ridiculous."

"Do you want to spend the night in somewhere like New Jersey or Ohio only for this airline to tell us it will be another week before they can get us on the next flight?"

Michelle considered her options and then pressed the call light.

The attendant seemed annoyed that another passenger wanted his attention at a time when he was considering whether to completely ruin the day of several hundred passengers for a first-time flier's overreaction. Still, he dutifully made his way down the aisle toward us.

The woman could still be heard hyperventilating behind us.

"Yes, ma'am, can I help you?" asked the attendant.

"No, actually I think I can help you. I'm a nurse. Is the lady behind us all right?"

"Oh, yes, ma'am. I think she's just having a panic attack. She's a first-time flier."

"Would you like for me to check on her?"

The attendant turned his attention to the troublesome couple behind us. "Folks, this lady here is a nurse. Would you like her to check you out?"

"I think she'll be fine," said the man.

The woman began hyperventilating louder.

"Are you sure?" asked Michelle.

The woman continued to hyperventilate. I glanced between the gap in the seats and saw her meekly nodding up and down.

My patience was about out. I should have been home by now, I had not had a decent meal in over a day, and more importantly, I did not have an appropriate amount of sleep or coffee to make me capable of functioning in the world of people.

I yelled over the seat. "Listen, lady, you need to either let my wife help you or pull yourself together. It's an airplane. It's routine. We're not being launched into outer space; we're just going to Charlotte. Calm the hell down."

Everyone looked at me. Absent was any comment from anyone. Also, and more importantly, absent was the sound of hyperventilating. Our first-time flier had gotten her shit together.

The remainder of the flight was uneventful. The thud as we touched down in Charlotte brought a great sigh of relief to both Michelle and me. We were not just in the United States, but we were back home in North Carolina. All we needed to do now was clear customs, retrieve our bags, and obtain a rental car to get us back to Raleigh.

Customs was more complicated than it needed to be with long lines and complicated forms. The agents all looked half asleep and perturbed with their jobs and, possibly, with our very existence. After a week of trademark Canadian politeness, the agents' attitudes were almost welcoming. It was good to be back home in the United States.

We were promised in Toronto that our luggage would arrive in Charlotte with us, but since there was no Air Canada counter in Charlotte, we were to retrieve it from its partner in what is called the Star Alliance.

The Star Alliance is a federation of airlines around the world that work together to ruin their customers' lives and cause the most inconvenience possible. In Charlotte, the Alliance partner was United Airlines.

I don't know why I had hope when I arrived at the designated baggage carousel. After all, Air Canada had been holding us hostage for over thirty-six hours at this point.

Predictably, my hopes were crushed when the last bag came down the carousel and our luggage never materialized. We went to the baggage office, which, even though it was a weekend and even though the airport was busy and crowded, was completely closed, unlit, and locked. "Welcome home, assholes," the empty office seemed to say.

By now, several other members of our flight were beginning to feel the stress of the situation and were yelling at the empty office. Some woman went to retrieve an airline employee at the ticket counter, which necessitated going to a completely different part of the airport.

An airline employee with a dour expression on his face made his way down the concourse toward the baggage claim area shortly thereafter. Inexplicably, *The Imperial March* began to play from somewhere in the universe as he walked. The employee arrived at the group of us all standing at the empty claim office and looked at the office momentarily. He then turned his attention back to us with an expression filled with indifference.

"It's closed," he said.

This man was clearly management, as he so deftly figured out the problem in record time.

"You'll have to call the 800 number and open a claim," he said. He then turned around briskly and walked off without entertaining any of the several questions the crowd was attempting to ask. I suppose we were lucky in this regard since this was United. He could just have easily beaten us and drug us out of the airport, or killed our dogs.

We had secured the rental car and were on the interstate toward Raleigh within thirty minutes. We were finally going home. In Vancouver, we had seen a multitude of bald eagles flying high above the city and elsewhere in the province. These majestic birds always caught our attention and made us feel American.

The United States is never to be outdone by Canada, however. Fireworks from small-town baseball stadiums periodically lit up the night sky along the interstate; the rocket's red glare and bombs bursting in air welcoming us back home.

The next day, my phone rang. "Mr. Banks?" asked a cheerful-sounding woman.

"Yes, this is him."

"I am calling from Air Canada in the Raleigh Airport. Are you still missing a bag?"

"Is there luggage there with my name on it?"

"Why, yes, sir. There is."

"Then I am still missing a bag."

"I see. I will have someone come out and deliver it today."

"That would be great, thank you."

Several hours later, a van pulled up to my house, and two burley men exited, carrying my suitcase. To be clear, it was just my suitcase. Michelle's was nowhere in sight.

"Here's your bag, man," one of the men said as he handed me my suitcase.

"Thanks," I said. "Where is the other one?"

"It's at the airport."

"Why is it at the airport?"

"We ain't had no paperwork."

I stared at him with curiosity.

Sensing my bewilderment, he continued.

"See, man, we saw the bag. It was right next to this one. Saw the tag said 'Banks' and had the same address and everything. But the airline, they didn't give us no paperwork for that bag. They only gave us paperwork for this bag."

"Then how do I get my other bag?"

"They'll probably send us the paperwork later today, and someone will bring it by here tomorrow."

"Can't I just go by the airport and pick it up myself?"

"No, sir. We have to bring it to you."

"I guess that makes sense," I said, even though none of it made sense. En retard, again.

It rained overnight—not a small drizzle or even a summer shower but the type of rain that unleashes flash flooding in some areas and drenches everything completely. Thunder helped round out nature's soundtrack, and the lightning provided the pyrotechnics for the symphony.

Given this meteorological show, it came as no surprise to me when I opened my front door in the morning to retrieve the newspaper and found Michelle's suitcase on the front porch. Someone from the airline had dropped it off in the early morning hours while everyone else was sleeping.

I suppose it was courteous of them not to ring the doorbell and wake us. Although the necessary consequence of this action was that Michelle's suitcase was now completely saturated with rain water.

I found that I could not even will myself to be angry by the soaked suitcase now dripping a sizable puddle on my floor. The Canadian Hostage Crisis had finally come to an end.

Not So Gently Down the Stream

I grew tired of sitting on our cabin's porch and staring into the trees while we were vacationing for a week in a small town just outside of Asheville. Somehow, I was able to convince Michelle to spend a day whitewater rafting on the Nantahala River. She is not a nature person, or even an adventurous person, so naturally she had reservations. Was it safe? It isn't too dangerous, is it? I reassured her by lying.

Whitewater rafting is a sport where eight people and a guide pile into what amounts to a pool float on steroids and launch themselves into a fast-flowing angry river filled with rocks and who knows what else. The oars, they warn you, must be held tightly at all times, and one is to never, ever let go of the t-grip at the end. If you do, you could either knock yourself unconscious or knock someone else's teeth out. A helmet is required, for at any moment you could plunge over the side and smash your head on one of the boulders.

A life jacket is also required, but the rafting guides call it a personal flotation device because the term "life jacket" is misleading. It implies there is some guarantee you will live. If you were to go into the water, you would surely float, but your legs may get caught on a submerged branch or even some rocks. Then, the river's powerful current will push you forward and over; your face stuck in the water until you drown.

Whitewater rafting is less safe when I am on the raft. This is not because I cannot follow the directions of the guide or have no aptitude for the task. It's just that I have bad luck. I had been rafting only two times prior, and both times involved less than desirable events.

A snake was seen swimming gracefully through the river on my first rafting expedition. All of us turned to watch it move effortlessly through the river perpendicular to the raging current. And by all of us, I mean the guide was looking at the snake, too.

I turned my attention away from the snake briefly and looked forward. Straight ahead was a large amount of water being lifted briefly into the air before returning to the rest of the river, like a sort of massive drinking fountain. *That's weird,* I thought. *Why is the water lifting out of the river like that?*

"Rock!" I yelled.

The guide and everyone else turned their attention forward again. It was too late to do anything, and we slammed into the boulder with a jerking thud. My side of the raft caved in, and I found myself suddenly in the water with three of the other people in the raft.

Keep your feet up, I reminded myself.

I began to drift with the current and away from the raft. Amazingly, I still had my paddle in my right hand. The raft dislodged itself from the rock and began floating with the current as well with only half of its occupants and the guide remaining.

The guide was shouting directions to the four remaining passengers to steer the raft toward the four of us in the water. The raft was picking up speed as they paddled, and I saw them begin plucking the other three out of the water one by one.

I began using my free arm to paddle toward the raft. I grabbed the side of it once I reached it while the rescue efforts continued. Holding on to the paddle with my left hand and the raft with my right, we continued down the rapids.

My butt hurt. We were floating over submerged rocks and branches that were not deep enough to avoid me grazing the tops of them. In more ways than one, the river was kicking my ass.

I began to feel myself drift under the raft once we were in a calmer part of the river. Suddenly, both my feet and most of my abdomen was under the raft. I swung my left arm and grabbed the side of the raft, throwing my paddle in.

I felt hands on my life jacket, and I was yanked in one swoop into the raft as if I were some sort of game fish. I flopped around the deck of the raft as we continued and almost bounced back into the water when we hit a particular set of rapids. Eventually, I regained my seat and kept rowing.

_____

The second time I went whitewater rafting was less hazardous for me. I cannot say the same thing about the others on my raft, however.

We were about halfway through our trip down the river when the guide on this voyage indicated we were going to do some surfing. Growing up on the coast, the only surfing I was familiar with involved waves, a board, and a level of balance and coordination I most certainly did not possess.

"The hell we are," I mumbled under my breath. There was no way I was going surfing down a river.

As it turns out, surfing in rafting parlance is different. It involves something worse.

A hole in rafting terminology is a feature in a river wherein the water passes over the top of rock. As it flows over the obstacle, it travels deep toward the bottom of the river and then reverses back onto itself. This essentially creates an aquatic hamster wheel. Larger holes can actually stop and flip a raft. However, smaller and less powerful holes can be used to "surf" the river where the raft rides stationary over the top of the water.

We steered ourselves toward the hole and rode the current into the top of it. I must admit it was kind of fun riding the cyclical wave and bouncing with it.

I looked across the raft, and there was a young woman who looked scared. Thin, blonde, and soaked as she was, she weighed maybe a hundred pounds. As the bouncing continued, the woman's position in the raft became more precarious to the point where it looked like she would be bounced into the hole. I reached out to grab her life jacket and pull her into a more secure position on the raft.

I missed. I felt the woman's arm on the palm of my hand but failed to close my fingers around it in time. I was staring at an empty seat a mere second later.

Oh shit, I thought. *I just pushed that lady into the river.*

I looked around quickly, in a panic. Fortunately, all of the other passengers and the guide seemed to be focused on keeping the raft on the churning water and didn't seem to notice that I may have just killed one of our fellow rafters.

"Man overboard!" I yelled.

Everyone turned to look. We could see the woman flailing about and trying to keep her head above water. The hydrodynamics of a hole cause it to act as a kind of aquatic clothes dryer, tossing whatever is in it in a constant loop. The woman was no exception.

The guide called out to her, and she signaled with a thumbs up that she had heard what he said. He then commanded a rafter on her side of the raft to extend their oar toward her with the t-grip on the woman's end. Once he did so, the woman grabbed it and clutched it with both hands, holding it so tightly her knuckles turned white. Of course, the white knuckles could also have been due to the frigid water.

With a heave and a ho, the woman was hoisted back into the raft and looked stunned while she coughed up some of the water that had made its way into her lungs. She was completely drenched and was likely already suffering the symptoms of post-traumatic stress disorder. She looked around wildly trying to ascertain what had just happened, still in shock.

After a minute or so, she resumed her seat on her side of the raft and picked up her oar. The fun of surfing the hole had ended, and the guide had us row off of it and continue on our journey down the river.

I could feel the woman staring at me as her adrenaline wore off and she came back to her senses. She undoubtedly had pieced together by now that I had for some reason pushed her out of a perfectly good raft into one of the worst experiences of her life. She must have thought I was an idiot, or, perhaps worse, a deranged and homicidal maniac. She would never know which.

I stared straight ahead the rest of our journey and avoided all eye contact. Once we were back on land, I quickly turned in my gear and ran to my car before the woman was able to relay what had occurred to her extremely muscular significant other waiting for us back at the drop point.

Michelle and I were staring out the window of the buses that were taking us to the put-in location while these fond memories replayed in my mind on the day we were to go whitewater rafting together. I could sense Michelle's trepidation.

"Are you sure this is safe?" she whispered to me.

"Oh, absolutely," I replied. I made a note to myself not to push her overboard, either by accident or on purpose.

The group that signed up for our trip was quite large, and we required two buses to transport everyone. Once we arrived at the put-in location, everyone disembarked and stood in a line.

"We're going to divide you up into groups of eight for the rafts," said one of the guides.

"How many of you have rafted before?" asked another.

Only two of the forty of us raised our hands.

The guides, all five of them, then formed a huddle and began talking quietly among themselves, glancing over the crowd as they did so.

They broke from their huddle and started pointing to random individuals.

Michelle and I stood there as we watched thirty-five strangers be picked one by one and begin to form smaller groups.

I suddenly had flashbacks to gym class in middle school, where I was always picked last for everything because I had zero athletic ability. Why was I not being picked? I had experience rafting; surely, a guide would want someone with experience in his raft since it's less work and instruction for him.

There were five of us left after the other rafts had their crews. Michelle and I stood next to a dainty middle-aged woman who appeared to be fast approaching her golden years. This made three of the eight that were to be in our raft.

The other five raftmates came in the form of two rotund men who I imagined would eventually be featured on an episode of *My 600 Pound Life*. I looked over at the raft and questioned how long it would be before we sunk and Michelle ultimately divorced me.

Once we made our way to the raft, the guide stared at it and us, his crew, with befuddlement as he attempted to figure out how to balance out the raft so we would not capsize in the first set of rapids.

I wondered what he must have done to get stuck with our raft while he performed the calculations in his head. Was this first day hazing? Had he slept with someone's sister? Also, why do I always get put in these situations?

My self-debate ended when the guide gave us our seat instructions. Toward the rear of the raft, next to him, would be the older woman. Michelle and I would flank the middle portion of the raft. Jabba the Hut and his twin would take the front two sides of the raft.

Michelle and I assumed our positions on the benches in the middle of the raft toward the outer hull.

"You should put your feet under the bench in front of you. It will help you stay in the raft when we hit the rapids," I said.

"I'm fine," she replied.

"Okay. Get thrown into the river if you want. What do I know? I'm only the one who has done this before."

Michelle has always been the smarter of the two of us.

A searing pain in my feet snapped my attention forward. One of the large men had taken his seat on the bench, which my feet were underneath. Both of the arches in my feet felt like they had collapsed and been crushed, how a bridge might behave if dinosaurs still lived and walked across it.

I struggled with all my might to pull my feet out, grimacing along the way. I tugged and tugged and tugged. I leaned back as far as I could, but the weight of the man in front of me had my feet trapped as if in a vice.

The pain was unbearable, but I knew I couldn't give up. I had visions of the circulation being cut off under the pressure and me becoming a double amputee after our two-hour trip down river.

I continued to struggle and fight to free my abused feet. Finally, they dislodged, and I thudded onto the raft's deck with both my legs sticking straight up into the air.

"You all right?" the guide asked.

"He done slipped right off the bench. Ain't bode well for the river," said one of the oblivious men.

I sat myself back on the bench, this time with my throbbing feet free. I would take my chances with the river. I glanced over at Michelle, who was smiling smugly.

I held my breath as we got underway and waited for us to sink no more than a few yards into our trip. The raft stayed afloat by some miracle.

The thing about rafting is one must be able to pay attention to directions. The guide commands each side of the raft to paddle at certain times to make sure we successfully navigate the rapids and stay in the raft.

The two large men were incapable of following directions. If the guide commanded the right side to paddle three strokes, the man on the left would paddle two strokes and the one on the right would do nothing. Navigating the initial portions of the rapids involved mainly myself and the guide using all our strength to prevent disaster.

The man in front of me also seemed to have a hard time understanding that the paddle can turn into a weapon if not handled properly. I spent most of our trip down the river dodging the t-grip flying at my head and debating whether to just throw myself in the raging river as a more efficient use of my time.

Our guide bragged a bit while we were in a more mellow part of the river. "I've been doing this for five years, and I've never had anyone go into the water," he announced.

I looked around our raft at the elderly lady, Michelle, and the two mammoth monuments of obesity in the front of the raft. There was a first time for everything.

We approached the gnarliest portion of the river, and I began to pray. *Please, Lord,* I said to myself, *do not let these two men go into the river during this stretch of rapids.* I knew that if they did, the elderly woman and Michelle would not be of much use, and the responsibility of pulling one or both of them out of the river would befall to the guide and myself. It would be the equivalent of trying to lift a VW Bug from a pool.

As we entered the rapids, the guide began screaming with a furor. The roar of the river increased exponentially as did the amount of water spraying and splashing at us from every direction. The raft bucked like a mechanical bull.

"Right three!" screamed the guide.

I used all my strength to paddle three strokes in the raging river. I glanced over my shoulder, and the guide had slid toward the right side of the stern and was doing the same. The boulder of flesh in front of me was clutching his paddle and looking around bewildered, not doing anything.

"Left four!" screamed the guide again. He had slid quickly to the left side of the stern, almost knocking the elderly woman into the rapids.

Michelle paddled four strokes, the river rebuking her efforts, and she accomplished as much as someone sweeping dirt in the desert.

I glanced behind me again and noticed the other rafts in the expedition were beginning to enter the run. These rafts were filled with fit, athletic, and toned bodies

"Right five! Right five! Do it now!" the guide screamed.

There was a large boulder directly in our path. I strained to paddle five strokes, fighting the current while being bucked underneath from the river. Even the man in front of me was paddling.

Despite our efforts, we accomplished only a subtle change of course. The current was swift, and we were quickly approaching impact with the boulder.

"Remember to keep your feet up if you go in!" I yelled to Michelle, certain we would soon be in the river.

Or would we, I wondered? If we slammed head-on into the boulder with these two massive men in the bow, would we bounce off like a bumper car? Would the boulder smash into pebbles and the raft sail through, like an unstoppable juggernaut? In about thirty seconds, I would know the answers to these questions.

"Right six! Right damn now! Right six!" screamed the guide, growing hoarse.

We completed the sixth stroke of the paddles nanoseconds before we met the boulder. We had altered our course just enough to avoid a head-on impact, but the massive hunk of granite scraped down the starboard side of the raft, making an unpleasant sound as the thick rubber grazed the solid rock.

I was sure the boulder would punch a hole into the raft much like the iceberg did to the Titanic. Yet, somehow, we made it through unscathed and found ourselves in calm waters, adrenaline still coursing through our veins.

I turned to look over my shoulder and saw the other rafts, their guides shouting. The passengers were screaming. One by one, I watched as raft after raft flipped and sent its passengers and guides through the rapids. We paddled our raft sideways so the guide could make sure everyone got through the pass without becoming trapped on the wrong side of the boulder, or worse.

We continued down the river once all the other rafts were flipped upright and all passengers were safely returned. A short time later, we reached our destination and pulled near the shore where our buses were waiting. I could not believe that we had made it down the river without me or anyone in my raft being flipped into the river.

Both half-ton men swung up on the sides of the raft at the same time, putting enormous pressure on the bow such that it dipped lower in the river and some water came in. As soon as they were clear of the raft, the inflatable hull thrust itself back upward. The force pitched me over the side of the raft and into the water.

Of course, I thought. I planted my feet on the river bottom and stood upright, completely drenched and soaked from being momentarily submerged. Of course.

There's a High Probability We'll Be Murdered in Our Sleep

M ichelle's cousin was set to get married in Nowhere, Virginia, outside on a hot, sweltering Southern July weekend. We rarely saw Eliza, and when we did, it was usually while watching her cry over some teenage angst, even though she was an adult, or listening to her go on about the newest young adult book she was reading. This obligated us to attend the wedding. Because, family.

To be fair, I was not totally opposed to attending the wedding. Although I detest weddings in general, and especially weddings out of doors during a Southern summer, this one promised to be potentially entertaining and a spectacle. Most of the gatherings of Michelle's family tended to be spectacles, in fact.

We had met Eliza's fiancée, Elijah, the summer before at their engagement party in Richmond. He was a quiet guy, and I did not think I would have anything in common with him. He certainly did not seem to share any of my interests, as all he seemed to talk about was his biggest hobby, baking, and planning his wedding. Elijah did have a tendency to openly judge his future in-laws, however, which made him an all right guy in my book.

Nowhere, Virginia, does not have any hotels. As far as I could tell, the only thing it did have was the wedding venue, a stone conference center on the ridge of a mountain. A few trailers with Confederate flags hanging outside were also located in the town. The nearest hotel was thirty minutes from the venue, in a town called Dullsville. The single option for lodging was a Holiday Inn at 150 dollars per night.

I am an incredibly cheap person, especially when it comes to spending money on things I do not want to spend money on. There was no way I was going to pay 150 dollars to the hotel monopoly in Dullsville to attend a wedding I did not want to attend to begin with. After some online researching, I found a hotel only forty minutes from Dullsville in the neighboring town of Boondock.

Boondock was home to a mildly famous state park with a natural rock formation that attracted senior citizens and RV drivers from across the region. On the border of the park was an independently owned historic hotel that, from the pictures, looked attractive and luxurious, a throwback to classic hotels from the time of the Great Gatsby when luxury trappings were commonplace.

There were two obvious selling points to the hotel: (1) it was not the hotel where the rest of the family was staying; and (2) it cost half of what the other hotel cost per night.

We pulled up to the hotel, and everything seemed fine initially. The building was a colonial revival style of architecture with stone facing and elegant awnings. Porters stood at the grand entranceway with their traditional red jackets and the strange little hats that resemble an overturned bucket of chicken.

I was struck by the spaciousness of the lobby walking in and how it resembled an old-fashioned country club. We walked to the front desk to check in.

"Name?" asked the clerk.

"Banks."

She searched her computer for a second.

"Ah. Here it is. I have some good news and bad news."

This is never what I wanted to hear when traveling.

"Bad news first," I said.

"The main hotel is completely booked this weekend."

How the hell was anything in Boondock ever completely booked?

"But," continued the clerk (there is always a but), "We do have one of our cabins available. It's a five-minute drive, but you'll have a whole cabin to yourself."

This actually sounded promising. The clerk pulled out a map that showed the main hotel and the one road in Boondock. There was a small side road near the entrance to the state park that led to a collection of small cabins. If they turned out to be half as nice as the main hotel itself, this would prove to be the best hotel deal I had ever found.

We left the parking lot of the main hotel and traveled a short distance down Boondock's road. We kept looking for the side road but were unable to find it, and eventually we reached a sign that said "Now Leaving Boondock. Come back soon!" By eventually, I mean within a half mile.

We turned around and drove the other direction down the road. We still could not find the side road before I reached the main hotel again. I pulled over and consulted the map.

"It's definitely that direction," I said pointing toward where we had just come. "Did you see anything?"

"No," said Michelle. "The only thing I saw even close to a road was that gravel driveway that led back into some woods."

We both looked at each other for a moment in silence. I turned the car around and drove back down the road, this time turning onto the gravel driveway. We soon came upon a clearing with a cluster of a half dozen cabins arranged in a semicircle.

The cabins were surrounded by forest and rustic, but not in the stylish way you might see in an affluent mountain community or gracing the pages of a Pottery Barn catalogue. These cabins were rustic in the sense that they looked like they had been abandoned since the last century and may not have indoor plumbing.

We found our particular cabin and pulled in front of it. The porch had not been swept, the siding looked half rotten, and the screen door was hanging by a single hinge.

"Are you sure this is right?" asked Michelle.

"It has to be the place. I guess we'll find out when we try the key."

We exited the car and approached the cabin with some apprehension. I gingerly opened the screen door and inserted the key we had been given into the lock on the flimsy wooden door. I prayed the key would not work and this was all a mistake.

I turned the key, and the door creaked open with a labored groan.

"Shit," I muttered.

Michelle was only in my peripheral vision as I opened the door fully, but I could still see she was pissed, and I didn't dare make direct eye contact. I knew already that at least a dozen times this evening I would be reminded and scolded that we should have stayed at the hotel in Dullsville with the rest of her family.

"Wait here," I suggested to Michelle.

"Why?"

"Let me check it out first. You know, to make sure there's not a rabid raccoon or a crime scene or something inside." I thought a little humor might help diffuse the mood.

Michelle turned around without saying anything and walked back to the car, taking a seat inside. *Click.* She locked the doors behind her.

The stench of mildew and mothballs struck me as I entered the main room of the cabin. To my right was a queen size bed with some kind of floral-printed bed covering from the 1980s. A scratched wooden nightstand held a lamp with a dingy shade and what was perhaps the first model of push-button phone ever manufactured.

To my left were the closet where a body was possibly hidden and the bathroom that was lined completely with a light green tile from floor to ceiling and a pedestal sink that had seen better days.

I turned back around and waved Michelle the all clear. She climbed out of the car and grabbed her luggage.

"It's not so bad," I tried to reassure her.

"Shut the hell up and get your stuff. We have to leave for the wedding in thirty minutes."

The drive to Nowhere took us back through Dullsville and past the Holiday Inn. I glanced over at the passenger seat and saw Michelle staring at the hotel longingly.

The drive seemed to take forever as we wove our way through the Virginian foothills and into the mountains. The scenery along the drive was nothing but forest.

We reached the top of the mountain, and a sprawling stone event center with a large covered patio was before us. The structure looked like a mountain mansion for a rich celebrity, or possibly the meeting place for evil geniuses. My mother-in-law was here somewhere, making the latter more of a possibility.

The problem with having weddings at the same venue as the reception is that nothing is ever ready on time. We could not go into the structure because the staff was still setting up the reception area. This was the area that was air-conditioned. We also could no go out onto the covered main patio that had ceiling fans and views of the sprawling Blue Ridge Mountains because it was not time to be seated for the ceremony. Thus, we all stood around on the front patio in our suits and dresses baking in the late afternoon heat and beginning to look like we had just taken a short dip in a swimming pool thanks to the South's trademark humidity.

We were seated once everyone was miserable. The ceiling fans on the patio offered little respite and mainly circulated the muggy air, creating a slight breeze reminiscent of opening an oven. I stared off in the distance at the mountain range and thought about just throwing myself off the edge of the cliff we were on to end the suffering.

The groom took his place in front of the crowd, and the prelude began to play. His hair was immaculate, his skin fine, and his tuxedo was a deep navy blue with a lavender tie. Some type of water was streaming down his face, and it was difficult to tell whether it was simply sweat or whether he was already crying two minutes into his own wedding.

The question was answered for us when the bride made her appearance, and the crying turned into ugly sobbing. The bride took her place at the altar and was smiling but not crying. This was a strange reversal from the typical wedding.

I discreetly pulled out my iPhone and began browsing Facebook and the Internet at random, thinking about all the places I would rather be and all the people I would rather be with. Once my idle browsing was done, I turned my attention to reading the digital edition of *Outside Magazine*, my favorite periodical. One of the stories in the issue was titled "Murder on the Appalachian Trail," which was not far from where we were staying.

My focus on reading the details of what would likely happen to us later that night in our wooded cabin was broken by the strangest, most horrible sound. Some creature was wailing, its shrill screams sounding somewhat like nails being drug down a chalkboard. The tone and pitch of the creature was changing rapidly in an almost rhythmic way, which I found odd.

"What is that," I whispered to Michelle. "Do you think a coyote caught a raccoon and is killing it?"

"That's my mother's aunt, the soloist," replied Michelle. "She's singing *Ave Maria.*"

I glanced over my shoulder, and at the back of the patio I saw a woman pretending to be an Italian opera singer. I turned my attention back forward and thought about how much luckier the mauled raccoon would be in that moment.

Once the bride and groom said "I do" and walked back down the aisle together, the guests were left to continue roasting on the patio while the newlyweds took their wedding pictures. Just before we all died from starvation and dehydration, the event staff announced that the reception was to begin and we could make our way inside.

The reception was typical for a wedding. There was the traditional awkward mingling among guests, trying to figure out how they were related and if they were related at all. Toasts and stories were told of the bride and groom that somehow are supposed to make a wedding more intimate as if you had not just witnessed the couple kiss in public and become legally obligated to each other for eternity—or until the divorce, whichever came first. There was drunken dancing by white people, or, more appropriately described, ungraceful jerking and convulsing off beat.

The booze made it more bearable. It should be illegal not to have alcohol at a wedding as it serves a vital function. It is not just to make the customs, traditions, and bad deejaying more bearable, but it makes the horrendous food more palatable. This wedding, like all others before it, provided a buffet of catered slop meant to pass as an elegant spread of fine food: the shoe leather beef with mushroom gravy from a dog food can; the tough plastic-like meat labeled chicken with some mystery cream sauce; day-old stale dinner rolls; and a variety of vegetables cooked to various levels of doneness between raw and completely limp.

The bride and groom were whisked away in a rented Rolls-Royce down the side of the mountain at the night's end after running precariously through a tunnel of combustibles we were forming with sparklers in our hands. I never understood this custom in a wedding. It would seem more logical to use rice and risk a bird's health than to give drunken wedding guests fireworks in tight formation.

We drove up the dirt road to our cabin for the night. Seeing the place illuminated only by the headlights of my Jeep in the pitch black darkness of the forest did nothing to make the cabin more quaint or attractive and only heightened our anxiety.

As I pulled up into the front of the cabin, I saw something scurry off around the side of it. I was able to catch just enough of a glimpse to see it was a large opossum, which I suppose was fine as long as it stayed outside of the cabin and was not inside.

I climbed out of the Jeep and heard rustling coming from the tree line. It was probably just a deer or perhaps someone waiting to murder us and steal our money and car. Only the next few minutes would tell.

"Are you getting out?" I asked Michelle, who was still seated and buckled into the front passenger seat.

"Not until you go in there and make sure it's safe."

I walked intrepidly to the front door of the cabin bound and determined to make Michelle believe I was confident in the choices I had made that had brought us here.

When I reached the door, it appeared to be slightly ajar. My heart began beating faster, and I wondered if a murderer was waiting for me, a rapist, or maybe just a black bear in search of food. I hoped it was the bear. That would seem more random and out of my control so that others would not say things like, "We told them to stay at the hotel in Dullsville" at my funeral.

I pushed the door open, stepping back slightly as I did. We had forgotten to leave a light on, so complete darkness prevented me from seeing anything that might be waiting inside. We had remembered to leave the porch light on, however, and so once the door was open, I saw a swarm of moths and other bugs fly across the threshold. They seemed eager to say hello to the termites and cockroaches I was sure infested the walls of the old cabin.

I stepped across the threshold with bated breath and reached along the dingy wall until I found the light switch and flipped on the light. When I did, a spark flew out of the wall from behind the switch, so I figured it was a good thing we did not leave a light on while we were away lest the cabin should burn to the ground and we returned to a smoldering ash heap. I didn't share this thought with Michelle, because I could sense she was already looking for an excuse to sleep in the Jeep or force me to drive to Dullsville and get a room at the other hotel.

When the light came on, I saw two mice scurry into the closet, but otherwise the room looked all clear. I motioned for Michelle to come inside. She was glaring at me from the Jeep. I couldn't tell whether she was upset again that I made her stay here or that I had not been murdered by some psychopath lurking in the cabin so she could collect the life insurance and not have to worry about her cheap husband any longer. Probably both.

We got undressed and pulled back the comforter and bed sheets and found ourselves pleasantly surprised that there were no insects crawling around. We both climbed into the bed, and the ancient springs creaked and popped under our weight. The lumps in the mattress felt as if I were lying on top of a ball pit in a Chuck E. Cheese restaurant.

I turned toward Michelle with a smile on my face. She was reading a book and ignoring me, consistent with our typical bedtime routine. I tried to make a move, figuring we had just been to a romantic wedding. Michelle slapped my hand with her book.

"Are you fucking kidding me?" she asked. "Not in this place. It's filthy."

"Come on then. Let's get dirty."

"I'm already dirty from laying in this poor excuse for a bed in this dilapidated shack you're making me stay in. The answer is no."

I turned over onto my other side and turned off the table lamp. I had been asleep about an hour and a half when I was hit hard by a fist. I woke with a start, certain that this would be the end of my life.

Michelle had hit me.

"Wake up," she commanded.

"Why," I said groggily.

"Because I'm ready to go to bed."

"Okay? And?"

"And one of us needs to stay awake and keep watch."

I stared at her blankly. "What are you talking about?"

"Look at this place. Look at this place you've brought me to. This is some abandoned cabin surrounded by a forest. One of us needs to keep watch in case this is a trap. You've seen enough crime documentaries and thrillers to know that."

"Why can't you stay up and keep watch then?"

Michelle gave me one of those looks for which wives are famous. "You know why."

I sat up in bed and rubbed the sleep from my eyes while Michelle turned off her table lamp and prepared to fall asleep.

"How long do I have to keep watch?" I asked.

"Until I wake up," Michelle replied.

I knew better than to argue or protest, especially when Michelle was tired and someplace she did not want to be. It was better to take my chances with a homicidal maniac.

Is It Still Romantic if You End Up in the Hospital?

———

We spent the day walking around downtown Charleston on our babymoon. It was mid-June, so the South Carolina heat was oppressive. Occasional rain showers helped cool things temporarily but also made things more miserable as the humidity increased afterward. It was the perfect day for a pregnant woman who already felt miserable to walk for miles.

For those of you unfamiliar with the concept of a babymoon, allow me to enlighten you. It is a trip an expectant couple takes a few months before their baby is to be born. It is one last hurrah as a twosome where you can do what you want and when you want before your life is completely disrupted and you become a slave to a tiny human dictator.

The trip usually occurs toward the tail end of the second trimester or the start of the third trimester. Most of the preparations for the arrival of the baby have begun by the time a babymoon occurs: the registering for all the gadgets and necessities one pretends to know what to do with but in reality has no clue, the painting of the nursery, and the applications to the "good" daycares. It is the last panicked getaway for romance while the two of you think in tandem, "Oh, fuck, what have we done?"

Michelle and I had been to Charleston several times in the past and had already done most of things tourists come to see in the old colonial city. We had stared at the 1,500-year-old Angel tree. We had gone on a ghost tour in one of the supposedly haunted cemeteries. We had been to the old slave market that has been converted into a flea mall where you can buy all manner of cheap trinkets and overpriced T-shirts adorned with pictures of the palmetto tree. And, of course, we had been on a carriage ride drawn by horses and had taken pictures in front of old buildings and houses.

Having done most of the traditional tourist activities on our previous trips, we decided to have a new Charleston experience. This was less by choice and more by necessity given Michelle was just entering her third trimester and had a very noticeable baby bump. Some people on vacation tour fancy restaurants with celebrity or award-winning executive chefs. Others tour well-known bars and breweries. We toured a variety of public restrooms throughout the city due to the pressure on Michelle's bladder and rated their cleanliness.

We had unexpectedly found ourselves in the hospital back home in Raleigh a few weeks before our trip. Michelle had been having frequent and unexpected contractions, a sign of early labor. In the emergency room, her doctor checked her over and found the baby, a boy, was healthy and normal and speculated that Michelle was pushing herself too hard, not drinking enough water, and needed to take it easy. She had been working full time as a nurse while completing her master's degree at night.

Taking the doctor's orders seriously, we walked a collective ten miles in the heat of a Southern June on a single day in Charleston. I did wear a CamelBak, however, and made Michelle drink from it every ten minutes or so to remain hydrated as the doctor suggested. This, of course, only exacerbated the need to find a restroom every fifteen minutes.

We grew hungry as dinnertime approached, and we made reservations at a small, local restaurant that strangers on the Internet told me I would love. This is the type of place we like to eat, especially on vacation because it allows us to try new culinary experiences and support the local tourism industry rather than a national corporate chain. Of course, the fact that these places are generally less crowded and largely free from tourists are the primary reason we go because we don't like people.

Michelle had started complaining that she needed a break by the time we walked into the front door of Elliot's Table, and the restaurant seemed like just the place. It was intimate with not much room for large crowds. The menu was a single page, with a handful of options, and the waiters wore professional-looking uniforms without nametags. We knew this place would be classy and expensive. It was exactly the type of place to rest and eat while wearing shorts and T-shirts stained with sweat after walking around outside all day.

Our table was situated in the middle of the room, and I noticed everyone staring at us as we made our way to it. Perhaps it was our appearance. "Shouldn't you be at the The Crab Shack?" the looks on some of their faces seemed to say. More than likely, however, they were staring at Michelle who was by now flush-faced and breathing a little heavier. The sweat made her maternity dress stick to her sizable baby bump, enhancing her pregnant appearance and making it look like she was further along than she really was.

Michelle does not seem to notice when people stare at her in public. She has always been attractive, and most of the people who stare at her are men. I almost always notice when people look at Michelle, or me for that matter, because people cannot be trusted. You have to keep an eye on them. Since Michelle had been pregnant, I noticed men and women, young and old, staring at her everywhere she went.

There was a mother and her college-aged daughter at the table next to us when we sat down, and I noticed their stares right away. They were the type of stares that are accompanied by large, bulging eyes. They undoubtedly thought Michelle could go into labor at any minute and appeared worried about getting something on their high-dollar pumps when the water broke.

The waiter was particularly attentive, which is customary in these relatively small restaurants. He gave us a few minutes to peruse the small menu after taking our drink orders.

The waiter was eager to tell us about the evening's specials, which included a chicken dish that was described as succulent and incredible.

"I'll have the salmon," I said.

"Actually, the chicken special sounds delicious, I'll have that," said Michelle.

"I'm so sorry, ma'am," said the waiter. "We're out of the special."

"But you just recommended it," said Michelle.

"I know. We're required to tell our guests about the special, but we sold the last one about five minutes ago," said the waiter.

"Um, okay," said Michelle. "I suppose I'll have the steak then."

"Sure thing. I'm really sorry you couldn't have the chicken; it really was delicious."

"Okay," said Michelle. "The steak will be fine."

"I eat chicken all the time," continued the waiter. "What I like to do is go to the grocery store and buy a rotisserie chicken and then use that in various things throughout the week. I'll use some of it to make a salad, some more of it to make a quesadilla. You're really limited only by your own creativity."

We both just looked at the waiter until he finally left for the kitchen.

I glanced around the room and noticed most people were still staring at us. The mother and daughter beside us were paying particularly close attention.

I turned my attention back to Michelle, who was breathing harder and was more red-faced.

"Are you okay?" I asked.

"I think so," Michelle said. She was unconvincing.

The waiter returned to refill our waters, hovering longer than before with a look of concern crossing his face as he looked at Michelle.

The mother and daughter glanced at us again then quickly glanced at the waiter as if to say, "Our meals better be complimentary if she goes into labor right next to us."

Once the waiter left, Michelle and I went about preparing to enjoy a nice dinner out in the way that most couples who have been married for many years do: we stared at our iPhones without speaking to each other.

"Are you sure you're okay?" I asked again after a few minutes.

"I'm fine," Michelle said.

I had been married to Michelle long enough to know when she says she's fine, she's not fine. Usually, she's mad at me. This time I suspected it may be different. The only thing I knew for certain, however, was that it was never wise to argue with her when said she was fine, regardless of the circumstances.

Our food came. About three bites into the meal, Michelle looked worse than she had a few minutes before.

"I need to excuse myself," she said.

"Are you going to be okay?"

The mother and daughter were now watching us with rapt attention, as were several of the other tables around us.

"I don't think so," she said.

"Do we need to leave?"

"I don't think so. But I'm going to go to the bathroom."

Michelle pushed away from the table and excused herself.

Everyone was looking at me once she had left the dining room. "Should you be doing something?" their looks seemed to inquire. I thought the same thing.

I knew Michelle was not fine, despite her assertions, so I flagged the waiter down, and he came dutifully over to the table.

"I need the check, please."

"Is everything all right, sir?"

"No. She's having an emergency in the bathroom."

His eyes grew wide. I realized I had not properly articulated what was happening.

"She's not feeling well. She's in the bathroom," I said.

I'm not sure why mentioning Michelle's location seemed so important to me at the time.

"I...see...," said the waiter. "Would you like a box for these?"

"No, thanks." I handed him my credit card without waiting for the bill to come.

The waiter returned with the check and promptly left the table. At the same time, Michelle had emerged from the restroom. I hastily scribbled my signature on the receipt and stood.

"Do you want me to go get the car?" I asked.

"No. I can walk."

"We're parked three blocks away."

"It's fine."

"Is it more contractions?"

"Yes."

"Are you sure you don't want me to go get the car?"

"I said I'm fine, damn it."

Everyone in the restaurant was looking at us now. I could tell by some of their expressions that they thought I should get the car, or perhaps call an ambulance. No one was going to argue with the pregnant lady having contractions that wanted to walk three blocks in the summer heat, however. We were in a restaurant, not a mental health ward.

Michelle waddled quickly the three blocks to the car. I pealed out of the parking lot like a NASCAR driver.

In my decades of driving, I have certainly seen information signs along the highways alerting motorists to upcoming McDonald's, Wendy's, and Starbucks. I had also seen the blue signs signaling a hospital was nearby.

I never understood these signs previously. I just assumed if you were in a strange city and needed a hospital, you would call 911 and summon an ambulance. Yet here I was, speeding along the streets of Charleston, following the little blue signs to the local hospital.

I was immediately skeptical of the hospital because it was not fancy like the ones back home. Duke and UNC both have valet parking and other modern amenities to justify the enormous size of the bills you receive just for thinking about getting medical care. But this was the only hospital nearby.

I dropped Michelle off at the entrance of the emergency room, and she walked in on her own while I went and parked the car in the deck.

The gentleman behind the information desk stared at me with apathy as I excitedly tried to explain why I was standing in front of him a few minutes later.

"I'm with the pregnant lady who just came through having contractions; where'd she go?"

"Are you related to the patient?"

"I'm the father."

"You're the patient's father?"

"No, the pregnant lady that literally just came through here. I'm her husband. The baby's father."

"So you're the patient's husband?"

"Can you just tell me where you sent her? This is an emergency, hence, why we're in the emergency room."

The apathetic man stared at me blankly.

"Name?" he asked.

"Banks."

"I'll look up the patient in the system and let you know where to go. How do you spell that?"

"How do I spell Banks? Are you kidding? Where did you send my wife? She literally just came in like five minutes ago."

"Sir, you're going to need to calm down, or you'll be asked to leave."

"Banks is spelled B-A-N-K-S. Exactly as it sounds."

The information man typed away on his keyboard and stared at the screen.

"Labor and Delivery."

"I figured as much. Where would that be?"

The information man sighed deeply, annoyed at being asked to provide information.

I ran down the hallways of the hospital and up the stairs, skipping the elevator, to the labor and delivery ward after extracting directions.

I found Michelle had already been taken back into an examination room and was undergoing an ultrasound by the doctor when I arrived on the floor. To be specific, she was being seen by a resident intern while the real doctor supervised.

The nervous intern looked like someone who should be cast in medical soap, or perhaps gracing the pages of a fitness catalog. Blonde hair, blue eyes, chiseled jaw, and a physique that was flattering even in hospital scrubs. This male model with his hand up my wife's genitals didn't inspire much confidence within me.

Nor did the real doctor, for that matter. She did not appear much older than the resident and had wide, bright eyes like she guzzled a Red Bull every ten minutes. She spoke quickly and encouragingly to the resident, much like a cheerleader would. "Like, you're doing great. Super great. Is the cervix closed? Go in a little deeper."

The two doctors left the room after a few minutes to consult and examine the results of some tests they had sent down to the laboratory. I pulled out my phone once they had left the room while Michelle lay in the hospital bed staring at the fetal monitor connected to her.

"What are you doing?" asked Michelle.

"Oh, nothing."

"You're focused pretty hard on that screen considering what's going on."

"Fine. If you must know, I'm looking up the doctors online to make sure they don't have any action against their license or malpractice suits."

"Must you be difficult at every doctor visit you attend?"

"I'm sorry if I care about what happens to you."

The doctors came back in the room ready to deliver their diagnosis.

"So it appears everything is fine," began the attending. The resident stood beside her with a blank expression on his perfectly symmetrical face.

"What do you mean everything is fine?" I interjected. "This is the second time this has happened in the past few weeks. She's having bad contractions and signs of labor. It can't be dehydration this time because I made her drink water every ten minutes."

"I know!" said the attending cheerleader. "It's weird, huh? Like, sometimes this happens in pregnancy where a woman goes into false labor. I dunno why. No one really does. Just happens." She shrugged.

The attending continued, "The good news is, mom and baby seem to be fine. The cervix is closed, and the heart rate is strong. The little fella just seems really eager to get out of there and meet the world!"

Michelle, likely sensing I was about to interject again and lose my patience, cut me off. "Is there anything I should be doing?"

"Shucks, nope," said the attending. "Everything seems to be fine. You'll get this a few more times, especially in the last trimester. Obviously, if it becomes too concerning, come back and see us, but otherwise, just continue to take it easy, drink plenty of fluids, and do what you have been doing. We'll finish up your paperwork and get you out of here soon."

Walking to the car, I realized my unborn son was impatient and stubborn. It didn't matter whether it was time to come out or not; he was going to try to do whatever he wanted to do. In the process, he would annoy Michelle and make her miserable at regular intervals. Any and all doubts as to paternity in my mind dissipated.

It's Hard to Sleep with Sand in Your Ass

I used to dream of adventure, especially as a child. I longed to be like Tom Sawyer or Huck Finn. Floating down powerful rivers on rafts, exploring old caves, and sleeping under the stars were high on my bucket list when I was young.

The first time I can remember camping was at the beach when we lived in Guantanamo Bay. My family decided to camp out with some friends, who also had a son my age. Our campsite was set back slightly from the shore, but the roar of the waves still provided a loud soundtrack. The shade of palms kept our tents and campsite relatively cool. Once the sun set, we continued to play and gazed up at the stars. It was a magical evening.

It was not to be repeated because my parents decided they hated camping on the beach. It was sandy, they said.

I have since come to learn nostalgia plays tricks on our minds when we are adults. My memory of that trip long ago has been tainted by the passage of years and a romantic notion of what the night was like, focused only on the positives and ignoring all the negatives. I've come to understand this not from any information or correction provided by my parents but through life experience in foolish quests to recapture the feelings of that trip.

Over two decades later, I found myself nearing the end of my first year of law school. It was a miserable year and the first time in my life I had found myself away from a coast. My law school was located in the middle of farmland. The biggest store in the area was a Walmart, a half-hour drive away. In college, I lived less than five minutes from Wrightsville Beach, where I would go every single day when the temperatures permitted. In law school, I found myself late for class, having been stuck behind farm equipment on the rural roads. The change was off-putting.

I needed to escape rural North Carolina and thought it would be a good idea to go camping on the beach. I called a friend from back home, and he and his wife agreed that they could stand to get away as well. The only question was which beach? We settled on Cape Hatteras National Seashore.

The weekend came, and we were unprepared. I did not previously own a tent, so I went to Walmart and bought the cheapest one I could find. Tom and Jordyn did not have a tent, either, so I bought one that said it could sleep between three and four people. What I know now, but did not know then, was that in tent vernacular, "three to four people" really means "two full-sized adults of average weight and height." Jordyn was short and slender. Tom and I were the opposite.

We arrived at Cape Hatteras National Seashore not too long before sunset and checked in at the ranger station to secure a campsite. It was April, long before Memorial Day and the official start of the tourist season, so the Ranger told us we could have our pick.

We drove around the circular drive that contained approximately thirty or so sites on either side of the campground. We settled on one near the dunes and an access trail to the beach but also with a view of Bodie Island lighthouse off in the distance. The weather was pleasant, that rare week in North Carolina after winter where it's warm but not sweltering. The clouds were scattered, white, and friendly.

We pulled the tent out of the package and began setting it up. In the summer, the sea breeze off the coast is pleasant and cooling in the heat and direct sunlight. However, when one is on the beach and trying to set up a tent, it functions more like a wind tunnel. As we tried to lay the main tent compartment flat to stake it into the ground, the wind turned it into a gigantic windsock. It took the might of all three of us and considerable time to get it anchored down in the sand long enough to put in the poles to erect our shelter.

Tents are designed by assholes. Exhibit 1: they do not have roofs. Instead, every tent has a thin mesh covering and windows, and if one wants any privacy or protection from the weather, you must put on a rain flap. This is exceptionally difficult on the beach due to the wind. For a tent designed to sleep three to four people, the rain flap turns into a parasail threatening to lift you off the ground and out over the ocean.

We managed to secure the rain flap, again using all our might and energy. But there were only three of us, and there were four sides to the tent, so it was lopsided. Every attempt to straighten it was met with more wind resistance. We finally gave up. The only part still exposed was a small portion of the mesh window on one side, perhaps an inch or so in height. Not enough to make any difference, we concluded.

For the next hour, we enjoyed each others' company over beer and the burgers we grilled. There were barely any other campers in the campground, giving us a largely private beach.

Weather can change in an instant on North Carolina's Outer Banks. One moment, it lulls you into in a false sense of security with a gentle breeze and sunshine, only for torrential rain to follow in an instant.

Shortly after sunset, dark clouds obscured the moon, and it began to rain. It was not a strong rain, but we did not want to be soaked. We retired for the night and climbed into the tent, even though it was barely eight o'clock at night.

Since it was my tent, I climbed in first, followed by Tom and Jordyn. We all got situated and began to doze off. It was not long before I could tell Tom was asleep from his snores and Jordyn as well from her lack of movement.

I was just entering that semiconscious state between awake and asleep when the wind shifted. *Tap. Tap. Tap.* A steady supply of rain drops managed to find their way through the one-inch-high opening in the rain flap, which I unfortunately had managed to lay down beside. The water was pelting me steadily on my forehead and nose. Essentially, Mother Nature was conducting Chinese water torture on me. How dare I deign to enjoy its beauty by camping, the weather seemed to be telling me.

I tried to turn over, but Jordyn was facing me and breathing through her mouth, casting hot breath in my direction that smelled faintly of beer. Meanwhile, the rain was now slowly pelting the back of my head.

I turned to face the window once more and tried to make the best of it. Surely, the rain wouldn't last too long; it never does at the beach. Besides, it was better to have fresh air and a little water than a little water and no fresh air. I tried to ignore it.

The wind picked up. Consequently, the side of the tent began to bow in and smack me in the face, bring more rain water with it. *Flap. Tap. Flap. Tap. Flap. Tap.*

I couldn't take it anymore and crawled over Jordyn and Tom who barely moved. Quietly unzipping the tent's door, I stepped out into the steady rain and made my way up the small hill to the parking space. I unlocked the car and climbed into the passenger seat.

I glanced around, and everything seemed quiet in the campground. A flash of light caught my attention. Then another. Then another.

I looked to my right, and the Bodie Island light was making its circular rounds. Unfortunately, the car was parked directly in the path of the beam. I reclined the passenger seat all the way back, but it didn't matter. The light still managed to reach me.

I covered my eyes with my left arm and tried to sleep. Eventually, I drifted off.

I was startled awake by banging on the car window in the middle of the night sometime later. I tried to see what was happening, but the Bodie Island light temporarily blinded me.

"Let us in!" someone was yelling.

"Help! Open the door!" screamed a female voice.

As I came out of my sleep, I realized Tom and Jordyn were banging on the window.

"Let us in!" Tom shouted again. Jordyn continued to bang on the window.

My hand started for the door locks in the car's armrest. I hesitated and stopped myself. What was going on? This was the type of scenario I had seen played out a hundred times in horror movies growing up— a dark and secluded campsite without many people around, a storm, an unsuspecting couple asleep in their tent—I calculated at least a 95 percent probability a murderer was nearby. Typically, this scene occurs after the couple finishes having sex in the tent or somewhere else. If Tom and Jordyn had done that in my tent, then perhaps they deserved to take their chances outside.

I glanced behind the car and did not see a large murderer with a hockey mask approaching. Of course, it was difficult to see anything in the pouring rain, which appeared to have increased in ferocity. A bolt of lightning lit up the sky, and I could see the tent in the near distance, partially collapsed. Another bolt of lightning lit up the sky, and I could see the few other campers down the campground running for their cars.

"Let us in!" screamed Tom and Jordyn again in unison.

I unlocked the car doors, and the two jumped in as quickly as they could, dampening my upholstery. The least they could have done was grab a towel from the trunk first, I thought.

"It's crazy out there!" said Tom. "Do you think we should leave?"

"We're in a car. We'll be fine," I said.

The two looked doubtful as the rain turned to hail and dinged against the car. The lightning was growing in intensity. Tom and Jordyn continued to stare at me for direction as if I were the group leader and responsible for what occurred. To be fair, I suppose this trip was my idea, but I had never assumed responsibility as captain of the expedition. I turned over on my side and went back to sleep.

The next morning, we were awakened shortly after dawn by the sun rising above the horizon.

I got out of the car and stood in the damp sand, turning my attention to our campsite. It had been replaced by a pond.

The tent was completely submerged, having collapsed in the wind and covered by the rising rain water in the basin where we had managed to pitch it. The collapsible captain's chairs seemed to have survived okay. One of the three had fallen onto its side and was also under water, but the other two were still visible from the armrests and up. Our cooler floated while a seagull perched on it. The bird seemed to be staring at me with judgment.

I waded into the shallow end of the newly made pool and shooed the seagull off the cooler. It perched itself not far away, waiting to scavenge whatever it could find among our rubble. I grabbed a beer out of the cooler and cracked it open. It may have been only shortly after dawn, but there was no sense in not drinking since we had a lot of time before our stuff resurfaced and dried.

———————

It was several years before I tried camping on the beach again. I called Tom, and despite almost drowning in his sleep on the last trip, he agreed to accompany me again. Jordyn wisely passed. We needed more than just the two of us, however, as I remembered how hard it was to pitch a tent on the beach with the wind. I called my friend Zack, who readily agreed.

The three of us decided to camp on Ocracoke Island this time. A long drive and a ferry ride later, we drove into the National Park Service campground and arrived at our campsite. It was again sparsely populated, as we had chosen to go before the Memorial Day tourist rush.

I learned from the last trip and invested in a small backpacking tent that slept "up to two people," which meant it slept one American-sized person. That one person would be me, and Zack and Tom would have to share their own tent.

A trail leading over the dunes and to the shore began at the backside of our campsite. I decided to pitch my tent along the trail, as I thought it would be nice to be able to just step out in the morning and go to the beach to catch the sunrise.

I pulled my tent from the bag it came in and began attempting to spread it on the ground. Immediately sand was everywhere. I brushed as much as I could off, aided by the steady breeze that kept trying to fling the tent into the campsite next to ours.

I positioned myself in the center of the small tent and splayed out my extremities to keep it pinned down. I nailed the stake into the ground at one corner and then carefully rotated myself clockwise to the other three corners until all were secure.

I stood up and grabbed the tent poles, glancing at Tom and Zack to see if they were able to make any progress. They, too, seemed to be struggling against the wind but seemed to be getting everything nailed down. Perhaps this camping trip would not be such a disaster.

A few minutes later, my tent was fully erect, including the rainfly, which was perhaps the trickiest part. I looked over at Tom and Zack, who were still struggling with theirs.

I zipped down the mesh door of my tent and stepped inside, trailing sand behind me. I reached back out and pulled in my overnight bag, which brought more sand. By this point, the floor of my tent was beginning to resemble a sort of sandbox.

As I was trying to scoop out some of the sand and return it to the beach where it belonged, a gust of wind came up and blew it all back in and then some. What's worse, it collapsed a side of the tent. I pushed back against the wind, but there was no getting the now concave tent wall to go back to where it belonged. That's fine, I thought. I can sleep in an enclosed, partially collapsed sandbox.

I climbed back out of the tent and glanced down the campground. Our nearest neighbors were approximately five campsites down. It was a troop of Boy Scouts who had erected a small tent city that appeared fully functional. By this, I mean it looked like it could withstand a category five hurricane if need be. Fuck those kids.

Turning my attention back to our campsite, Tom and Zack had finally managed to get their tent fully set up and were both standing around it looking proud of their accomplishment. I was slightly jealous that a side of their tent had not caved in.

A second large gust of wind blew through the campsite, taking Tom and Zack's tent with it. It really was quite mesmerizing to watch the wind rip the tent from the ground, flip it end over end, and throw it three campsites away. Tom and Zack looked on in disbelief. I couldn't help but chuckle to myself. And to think I was jealous.

Zack and Tom ran down the beach after their tent while I perched myself on top of the picnic table and opened the first beer of the sunny day. I watched as they struggled to haul the tent back and stake it into the ground once more. Finally, our campsite was set up and complete. It took only three hours.

The sun was long set and two cases of beer had been depleted by the time it was time to retire for the night (read: pass out). I crawled into my tent and situated just so to get comfortable. It was a futile effort. My skin felt sticky from baking in the afternoon sun, and at least a few grains of sand covered every surface of the tent and every nook and crevice of my body.

Nevertheless, I focused on the melodic and rhythmic sound of the waves fluctuating with the tide and eventually drifted off in a sleep that could be described as anything but restful. Occasionally, a gust of wind would disturb the ocean soundtrack and make sleeping even more difficult. *Flap. Flap. Flap.* The sound of the rainfly and collapsed wall of the tent fluttering with the breeze was nature's version of a snoring roommate.

I heard a commotion at one point in the middle of the night, but it had grown so late I did not care. As best I could tell, I was not in any imminent danger of being murdered, so I turned over and tried to go back to sleep.

The next morning, it was time to pack up, and when I exited my tent, I discovered that Tom and Zack had already done most of that. Their tent was nowhere to be seen, and I turned my attention to my car where Tom and Zack were asleep in both front seats.

I walked around the car and saw their tent, no longer fully assembled, chucked into the back cargo area. I learned later that their tent had collapsed in the middle of the night, and they sought refuge in the car. This was becoming a tradition.

I climbed into the driver seat once we were ready to leave. The smell of body odor and beer farts assaulted me. The sun warming the inside the car to oven temperatures as we packed up the campsite only served to intensify the noxious aroma.

Driving onto the ferry, I pulled toward the side and parked the car. I couldn't stand the smell any longer, so I got out of the car to catch some fresh sea air mixed with the exhaust of all the cars loaded on the boat. Tom and Zack went to get out as well but found themselves unable to do so. I had parked so close to the side of the ferry bulkhead that it was impossible for them to get out. They had made their bed the night before, and they could lie in it.

Race Relations

———

Michelle's family has a reunion every year in August. They congregate in the town of Aarons Creek, Virginia, which is essentially a church, a graveyard, and nothing else. The population was 145 at the time of the 2000 Census count.

The biggest event in the town each year is the family reunion. Relations come from far and wide to congregate in a little shack across the street from the church, which serves as a banquet hall. They catch up with relatives, tell the same stories, and stuff their faces with the same poorly executed Southern recipes year after year. The gastronomical suffering never seems to end.

One year, we were tasked with arriving at the shack early and making sure it was ready to receive the family. I knew it would be the most horrendous family reunion I had been forced to attend as soon as we pulled into the small parking lot.

The church parking lot is usually abandoned on Saturdays when we hold the reunion, but this particular sunny day, it was filled with cars and a rather somber-looking hearse.

Michelle and I sat in the parking lot across the street from the church and adjacent to the shack and cemetery. We wondered why on earth the church would allow a funeral to be taking place on the same day the family holds its reunion.

Suddenly, the door to the church opened and black-clad elderly people filed out one by one.

The deceased was the next to come through the door in a shiny wooden coffin, flanked by somber pallbearers. They walked down the short staircase of the church and along the path toward the hearse. We sat in our car watching the procession with confusion and quiet shock. I assumed they would load the corpse into the hearse and drive to the cemetery.

They didn't. The pallbearers bypassed the hearse and began making their way through the small parking lot toward the street with the rest of the mourners. They stopped dutifully at the intersection and looked both ways up and down the road where seldom a car traveled and began to cross en mass. We looked on with horror in the car.

The procession continued to make its way across the street with the coffin in tow, and eventually, the surviving 144 residents of Aarons Creek were flanking our vehicle from all sides on their way into the cemetery. The deceased was now mere inches away from my car door.

"Why is there a dead person next to me?" I yelled.

"I don't know!" replied Michelle.

We continued to sit there panicking while the mourners just stared as they made their way past.

Eventually, the town of Aarons Creek completed their passage to the freshly dug grave toward the back of the cemetery. We sat staring straight ahead toward the shack for several more minutes.

The family began to arrive shortly thereafter. We stood in the small yard and watched as car after car pulled into the parking lot. Hugs were exchanged, and loud elated greetings were given.

I turned toward the cemetery and looked at the mourners, who were watching our gathering in the distance. I silently envied the deceased.

A Prius pulled up, and an aging baby boomer in a tie-dyed T-shirt hopped out. The man had a closely cropped beard, glasses, and somewhat shaggy sandy hair that was peppered with gray. This was Uncle Bob, an aging hippy, who strayed far from the traditional conservative family values.

He bounded up the drive toward the rest of us and took his place in the group standing next to elderly Uncle Dick, who was wearing a camouflage trucker's hat, white T-shirt, and denim overalls.

Uncle Bob was smiling bigger than usual, and everyone turned to look at him as he cleared his throat to get our attention.

"Hey, everyone! I am so excited to be here with everyone again this year! I am super stoked to let you all know that I've done quite a bit of research over the past year and have a surprise for all of you that I think you'll enjoy and find very interesting."

These were my in-laws. I knew I would not find the surprise interesting or enjoyable. I stared back over at the cemetery where they were now lowering the coffin into the ground and wondered if there was extra room in the grave. I then turned toward the road where something caught my attention.

A caravan of minivans was approaching fast in the distance.

My wife's family is an old family. At the ancestral home, the family loves to show off an antique sideboard in the dining room. This isn't just any antique sideboard, however. This is a sideboard that was proudly floated down the James River to save it from the damnable

Yankees during the War of Northern Aggression. They then will quiz you on Civil War history.

After Michelle's grandmother died, we traveled to South Boston to help go through her affects and clean out the house. I was going through a stack of papers and books with lackluster curiosity. Some of the items were interesting, like the Army Navy Hymnal from World War II. Others made me wonder whether hoarding ran in the family; for example, a stack of *South Boston Gazette* newspapers from 1954 with seemingly no relevance to anything. Then among the aged, yellow paper and books fell a single sheet the size of a large index card.

John, James, Jonathan, Henry, Annabelle, Charlotte. The list continued, and there were about twenty first names in all. The paper was older than the rest of the stack, weathered and frail. Barely legible at the top of the list of faded names was "1859."

I stared at the list of names a few more minutes before it dawned on me what I was looking at—an inventory of the family's slaves. My jaw dropped in shock, and I sat down in the nearest chair I could find. What the actual fuck?

———————

Four years later, I watched the minivans come to a synchronized linear stop. A small army of people began pouring out in matching purple T-shirts. The T-shirts read "Martin Family Reunion." I was perplexed, as this was my wife's maiden name, but I had never seen any of these people before.

Also, they were African American.

I looked to my right and saw Uncle Bob with a wide, stupid grin on his face. The rest of the family stood in a group staring at the caravan army trying to figure out what was going on.

"All right, everyone!" began Uncle Bob. "This is the surprise I was talking about! As most of you know, after Gran died, a list of the family's slaves was found among her things." I began to feel nauseous.

Polite smiles turned to frowns as the half dozen or so brighter relatives began to figure out what was going on.

"I took that list and put in a lot of long hours and hard work at the library, register of deeds, and Ancestry.com. Eventually, I tracked the ancestors of our ancestors' slaves down and found out they took our family's name and most of our traditions. In fact, they have their family reunion right up the road about an hour or so, on this same weekend every year. And so I invited them to join us, and, well, here they are!"

"Aw, hell," muttered Uncle Dick under his breath.

"Momma and Daddy are probably rolling over in their graves," whispered Uncle Danforth to no one in particular.

I was dumbfounded. Most of the other family was as well. Suddenly, the funeral off in the distance was making more noise than we were.

Uncomfortable introductions began once the initial shock wore off. The two Martin families began to intermingle and introduce themselves by name and their relation to other Martins. My introductions took one of three forms:

1. "Hi. I'm Jackson. I'm married in. I'm not a Martin."

2. "Hello, I'm Jackson. My family is from the North."

3. "Uh, hey, I'm Jackson. My ancestors were Yankees."

Then a Toyota Camry pulled up behind the minivans.

"Oh, look!" said one of the newly discovered relatives. "Tabitha was able to come."

Tabitha stepped out of the Camry with another individual who was carrying what looked like a professional news camera.

As it turned out, Tabitha was a film studies major at the University of Virginia and had decided that this reunion may be the perfect opportunity for a new documentary for her class. When it came time for me to introduce myself, she pointed the camera right at me, and I just stood there like a slack-jawed idiot while Uncle Dick scratched himself through his overalls in the background.

The awkward mingling continued until dinner was ready. Dinner is a summer southern spread served buffet-style every year: banana pudding, pie, baked beans, slaw, hushpuppies, watermelon, and fried chicken. We all got in line, chose our food, and ate together while Tabitha continued to film. The patriarch of the newly discovered relatives, Uncle Ben, sat on the porch outside and ate. He was the great grandson of one of the slaves before they were freed.

The rule is simple: everyone makes their way through the buffet line once, and then you are free to get up and help yourself to a second helping of whatever you choose. This is where I made the biggest fool of myself.

"Can I get you anything?" asked one of the new family members.

"Uh, um, no. I can serve myself when I'm ready. You don't need to serve me, but thank you." I awkwardly replied.

After I was finished several minutes later, I decided I wanted to get some more of my favorite foods. I turned to Tabitha and asked, "Do you want any fried chicken?"

Tabitha stared at me for a moment. I stared back realizing how that may have come across.

"Oh! I meant because that's what I'm getting! Not, you know, because..."

Everyone at the table was staring at me at this point, including Tabitha's cameraman with his camera.

———————

There was another family tradition the African American side of the family did not adopt. Since Uncle Bob decided not to mention his surprise to anyone, no one thought this year's tradition through and could not plan accordingly. However, because the universe sees fit to make my life as uncomfortable and calamitous as possible, I had a gut feeling what was about to occur.

I sat there at the long table staring at my empty plate and watch, counting down the minutes until we could leave and hoping what I thought was about to happen would not.

But it did.

This tradition comes after dinner. Every year, the historians in the family call attention to themselves and tell the story of a family ancestor to keep their legacy alive. Since the family is quite old, sometimes this can be interesting. Most of the time, it's actually quite boring.

This year's covered portrait was brought out, and the historian in the family stood at the front of the dining hall, cleared his throat to gain everyone's attention, and began to speak.

"This year, we tell the story of one of the family's greatest patriarchs: a successful farmer, businessman, husband, and father.

"He was also a war hero. Rising through the ranks because of his strategic acumen while earning the respect of his fellow soldiers, he eventually became a general in America's bloodiest conflict."

I wanted to crawl under the table and hide. The cover was lifted off the portrait, and there he was. The war hero. I thought I was about to pass out from shame.

"Yes," continued the historian, "Great-great-grandfather Jedediah ultimately came home defeated in the Great War of Northern Aggression, as he called it, but he served honorably and fought for the ideals and values he believed in so strongly: a limited federal government and the right of the states to govern as they saw fit. Today, we honor his memory and contributions to the family."

The side of the family that is typically present every year clapped at the presentation. The newly introduced side, Michelle, and I sat there in stunned silence. Uncle Ben had walked off the porch and toward the line of minivans.

"Thank you so much for having us," said Tabitha as she stood up from the table. "But we really should be going now."

Goodbyes were exchanged, and the line of minivans pulled away and drove off into the distance.

I was glad for a moment that we were next to a cemetery as I was certain I would die any moment from embarrassment.

Santa, Maybe?

———

S pectacular is the only word that can describe the view from the plane window flying into Jackson, Wyoming. The Grand Tetons appear as though they will scrape the bottom of the plane at any second. One feels as though the airline will play some documentary soundtrack to fit the experience, something majestic with drums and trumpets. This, of course, presupposes that you are one of those fortunate people who have good luck when you travel. I am not one of those people.

It was hard to enjoy the view from the plane when all I wanted to do was pry myself out of the airborne sardine can. My soundtrack did not include trumpets, although I'm sure I could have made that happen if I could contort myself to reach the iPhone located in the carry-on beneath the seat in front of me. The airline did, however, provide me with an interesting soundtrack made possible with the seat assignments of the gentleman directly ahead and the infant across the aisle.

The gentleman did not seem to understand that you cannot recline any seat located in a sardine can, and the infant seemed upset by the gentleman's ignorance. No, my soundtrack was not something from the National Geographic Channel. My soundtrack was something more from the National Child Abuse Hotline: Smack, Wah, Smack, Smack, Wah, Smack, WAH, SMACK, SMACK, WAH! I've never been happier to deplane before.

Once I finished letting out a huge sigh of relief that my luggage made it to the same destination I had, I was whisked into a slightly more spacious vehicle and began the short trip from the airport into town. My cab driver was a pleasant woman who took great joy in pointing out everything there was to see along the way. The mountains, the river, the mountains, some more mountains, and...oh, over there...see that? Another mountain. I'm sure I would have enjoyed the trip had the cab driver shown herself the speedometer and the correct side of the double yellow line dividing the highway.

Upon entering the town of Jackson, one immediately sees the town square. It is a pleasant-looking park with four entrances, each of which surprises you with rather large arches made of antlers. I couldn't help but stare.

Noticing my wonderment, the driver said, "Don't worry: no animals were harmed in the making of those arches."

"I'm glad, because the folks at PETA may take real issue with your town otherwise," I replied.

"No, seriously. Elk shed their antlers. Not one animal was killed to make those arches."

I was suspicious but took her word for it. I was actually quite pleased to gain this nugget of trivia, as this may explain why I never see horns on top of my mother-in-law's head. I wondered if the devil's tail works the same way.

A few minutes later, I was deposited at my hotel, The Painted Buffalo. The hotel had a large statute of a buffalo out front painted in a myriad of colors. This, as I unfortunately came to find out, seems to be the only thing that has been painted at the hotel in the past half-century. True to its namesake, the hotel was large, somewhat strange smelling, and infested with fleas. This place was no Hilton despite the price of the room, and I decided that spending the remainder of the day exploring Jackson would be preferable to spending it in the hotel.

Johnny Cash must surely have been referring Jackson, Mississippi, in his song, as I can't see why he and June would mosey on over to this town. Sure, the scenery is gorgeous, and they have some great bars, but the rest of the town is nothing but kitschy tourist shops. Want an overpriced fringe leather jacket? Perhaps a cowboy hat and matching boots? A dream catcher? What about a very large belt buckle? If you answered yes to any of those questions, well, sir, you are in luck in the town of Jackson!

Just wander into any store along any of the streets, and you can find all of the above, right next to the tourist T-shirts that turn you into a walking advertisement for the town. I really don't see why tourist destinations like Jackson spend so much money on advertisements when the tourons (part tourist, part moron) who visit them turn themselves into human billboards wherever they go.

As I wandered around town in and out of all the shops, I marveled at the fact that this town is still standing. As happy as the folks at PETA would be with the town's arches, they would be one mightily pissed-off bunch at the rest of the town. Riots would ensue if they ever discovered this place. There are dead animals everywhere. Deer heads, moose heads, mountain lion rugs, and, yes, you, too, can have your very own stuffed grizzly bear. If you find that a moose head is just too cliché for your dining room, then worry not, you can have a buffalo head instead. Walking through the town provided more startling experiences than a Halloween fun house. Every time you turn around, there is some very large dead animal staring you in the eyes. And those empty black eyes follow you.

Night finally came, and I wandered (actually, I think the appropriate term for this part of the country is "moseyed") back to The Painted Buffalo. Even though it was July, the temperature was a cool forty-five degrees. I decided to sit on the bench outside my room and gaze at the stars for a while.

It had been a long day of traveling and wandering, and after a while of sitting on the bench, I had begun to settle into a short summer's nap when next to me there arose such a clatter. Naturally, I opened my eyes to see what was the matter.

A rather large gentleman had just sat down. His broad face was hidden somewhat by long white hair and a large beard as white as snow. His eyes twinkled, and his smile revealed merry dimples. His cheeks were like roses, his nose like a cherry.

"How the hell are you?" he asked quite merrily.

"Fine," I replied hesitantly. "How are you?"

"Can't complain. Where're you from?"

"North Carolina," I replied. "You?"

"Alaska."

I began to wonder whether his house was made of gingerbread and inhabited by tiny little men who make toys for a living, or perhaps airplanes. His general appearance and red T-shirt certainly left open the possibility.

"You lookin' for some business or just pleasure," he asked as if he were a foreign customs agent. I realized much later that this question was not directed toward the purpose of my trip.

"Pleasure," I replied. "You?"

There was a long pause as he pulled out a cigarette and puffed until the blue smoke circled his head like a wreath. He stared off into space while doing so, and I assumed by his quiet self-reflection that he was in town to mourn the slaughter of his reindeer to make the town arches. After what I had seen all around Jackson in the stores, I was now convinced the cabbie was full of shit.

"I'm from here originally," he finally said, "I came all the way down from up north to see my mother. She had a stroke and is in the hospital."

"I'm sorry to hear that. I hope she'll be okay."

"That old bitch will be fine! Woman's too damn stubborn to die," he replied. The bench began to vibrate as his laugh shook his stomach like a bowl full of jelly.

I began to feel sorry, not so much for him, his reindeer, or his mother, but rather for the T-shirt trying as hard as its fibers could to stay together. The poor things were stretched so very far and wide.

Looking to change the conversation back to just pleasantries, I extended my hand and introduced myself. He shook it but didn't say anything in return.

"What's your name?"

"Does it matter?" he asked.

Well, screw you, too. I thought you were supposed to be jollier.

After an awkward silence, he leaned in closer to me, "You can find a lot of fun in this town, you know." The situation was made even more awkward by the rancid smell of his breath and his rotten brown teeth. I also for the first time noticed that the rosy appearance of his cheeks was due more to dust and grime than anything else. This must be what Santa looks like on meth.

Getting no reply from me, Santa leaned back over to his side of the bench and finished his cigarette.

Surely, he will leave now, I thought. Alas, no. Santa reached into his jeans pocket and fiddled around for an abnormally long time. Curiosity got the better of me, and I had to look over. I really wish I hadn't.

It seems that Santa had been adjusting a rather large candy cane he stored in his pocket. Or at least that's what I told myself later that evening so I could sleep with both eyes closed. He was looking at me, and when he noticed me glance over in his direction, he smiled with his droll little mouth and, with a wink of his eye and a twist of his head, motioned to his lap. His hand patted the leg closest to me suggestively.

Surely this wasn't happening. "I don't want anything for Christmas this year," I excitedly announced, "and I'm not going to be your Dancer, Prancer, or Vixen!"

"Huh?" he exclaimed.

I took advantage of his befuddlement and sprang from the bench, giving a whistle. Then away I flew like the down of a thistle. I heard him exclaim as I ran out of sight, "Wait! We could have a real good night!"

Don't miss out!

Visit the website below and you can sign up to receive emails whenever Jackson Banks publishes a new book. There's no charge and no obligation.

https://books2read.com/r/B-A-MRFT-MVQXB

BOOKS 2 READ

Connecting independent readers to independent writers.

About the Author

Jackson Banks is the pen name for a writer living in Raleigh, North Carolina with his family. He uses his real life experiences and adventures to create a variety of stories across multiple genres, including thrillers, humor, and romance.

When not writing or spending time with his family, Jackson enjoys a variety of outdoor adventure activities and cooking to stay inspired.

Jackson's debut thriller novel, *Alligator River*, is coming soon. Make sure to sign up for his newsletter for updates, sales information, and and other useful information.

Read more at https://writerjacksonbanks.com.

CPSIA information can be obtained
at www.ICGtesting.com
Printed in the USA
BVHW040859150722
642218BV00015B/20

9 798201 048952